ENNEAGRAM
EMPOWERMENT

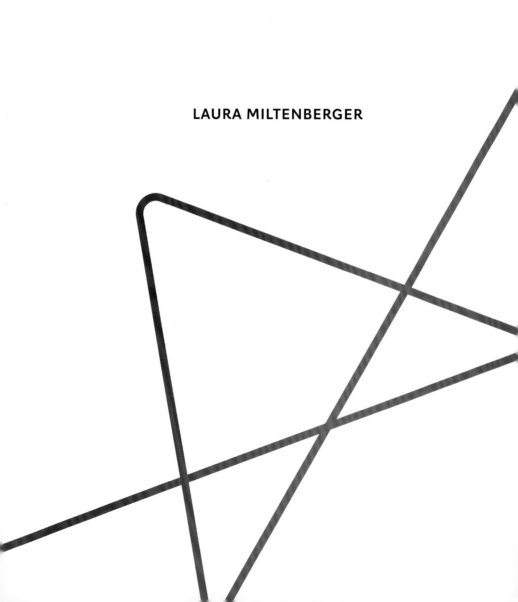

LAURA MILTENBERGER

ENNEAGRAM
EMPOWERMENT

Discover your personality type
and unlock your potential

Publisher Mike Sanders
Editor Ann Barton
Art Director William Thomas
Senior Designer Jessica Lee
Proofreaders Georgette Beatty, Polly Zetterberg
Indexer Brad Herriman

First American Edition, 2021
Published in the United States by DK Publishing
1450 Broadway, Suite 801, New York, NY 10018

A catalog record for this book is available from the Library of Congress.
ISBN 978-1-6156-4981-5

Note: This publication contains the opinions and ideas of its author. It is intended to provide helpful
and informative material on the subject matter covered. It is sold with the understanding that the
author and publisher are not engaged in rendering professional services in the book. If the reader
requires personal assistance or advice, a competent professional should be consulted. The author
and publisher specifically disclaim any responsibility for any liability, loss, or risk, personal or
otherwise, which is incurred as a consequence, directly or indirectly, of the use and application of any
of the contents of this book.

Trademarks: All terms mentioned in this book that are known to be or are suspected of being
trademarks or service marks have been appropriately capitalized. Alpha Books, DK, and Penguin
Random House LLC cannot attest to the accuracy of this information. Use of a term in this book should
not be regarded as affecting the validity of any trademark or service mark.

DK books are available at special discounts when purchased in bulk for sales promotions,
premiums, fund-raising, or educational use. For details, contact:
DK Publishing Special Markets, 1450 Broadway, Suite 801, New York, NY 10018
SpecialSales@dk.com

Printed and bound in China

For the curious
www.dk.com

To Margot and Mary Claire

Contents

PART 3: THE ENNEAGRAM AND RELATIONAL EMPOWERMENT

Introduction

The enneagram is not like any other personality test you have taken before. Because it doesn't just give you awareness of who you are now, in the present. It helps you pave a path toward who you want to become.

The dynamic system of the enneagram will give you the opportunity to invest in your strengths, compassionately work on your weaknesses, and understand yourself and your potential in a whole new way. If you want to become more confident in your ability to live life well, you need the deep kind of self-awareness that the enneagram can bring. And this is why the enneagram is so empowering.

What does it mean to be empowered? Well, do you remember what it felt like, as a child, when you were first able to see over kitchen countertops? Or first able to read and understand the world around you in a whole new way? Or first learned how to swim? Maybe you remember the first time you were strong enough to swing across the monkey bars, write your own name, or do a backflip on a trampoline. As you grew new muscles, gained more control over your body, and found new understanding of yourself and the world, you felt increasingly stronger and more confident in your abilities. This is what empowerment feels like. And this is really all that empowerment is; to be empowered is to become stronger and more confident in your ability to control your own life.

The enneagram is a tool that meets you right where you are and shows you who you have the potential to become. It can be utilized in all areas of your life. If you let it, the enneagram will help you grow new muscles, understand the world in a whole new way, and increase your confidence in your ability to live life well.

Enneagram Basics

Welcome to the enneagram, a tool to help you live life well.

What is the enneagram?

The enneagram is a nine-point personality-typing system. But it's not a typical personality-typing system, because it doesn't just describe your characteristics and traits. It goes much deeper than that, describing the driving forces behind your personality, like your core fears and motivations. And although the enneagram describes your strengths and virtues, it also addresses your weaknesses and obstacles to growth—the patterns of thought and behavior that are holding you back.

WHY IS THE ENNEAGRAM EMPOWERING?

Personal weaknesses can be difficult to accept, but when you realize which patterns in your personality are holding you back, then you know what you need to change in order to grow. Nothing is more empowering than when you take ownership of your whole self, along with all of your beauty and all of your flaws...when you use your strengths with confidence while still addressing your weaknesses to move toward maturity and growth.

WHERE DOES THE ENNEAGRAM COME FROM?

The enneagram symbol has ancient roots. But the contemporary understanding of the enneagram system derives from the mid-twentieth century teachings of Oscar Ichazo, a Bolivian spiritual teacher, and Claudio Naranjo, a Chilean psychiatrist.

HOW DOES THE ENNEAGRAM WORK?

The enneagram symbol has nine points, each describing a unique personality. One of these numbers is your dominant personality type, but all of the nine points of the enneagram are interconnected, accounting for the dynamic scope of personality and shifts in behavior that you have access to. For example, during times of security, you will have access to the traits of your security type. And during times of stress, you will have access to traits of your stress type. Rather than viewing yourself as static and predictable, the enneagram helps you understand yourself as you are, while showing you paths toward healthy change.

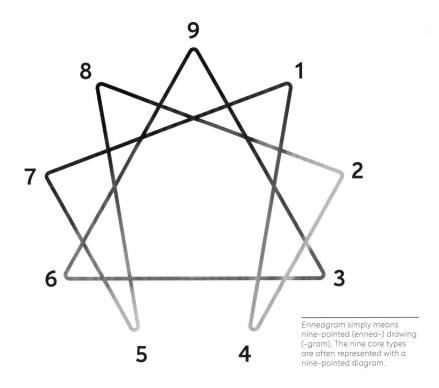

Enneagram simply means nine-pointed (*ennea-*) drawing (*-gram*). The nine core types are often represented with a nine-pointed diagram.

TYPE ONE
·········
THE VISIONARY
Perfectionistic
Conscientious
Rational

TYPE TWO
·········
THE CONNECTOR
Relational
Empathic
Helpful

Here's a sneak peek at the nine types.

TYPE THREE
·········
THE LUMINARY
Productive
Impressive
Competitive

What are the nine enneagram types?

The enneagram is based on nine personality types. Your dominant enneagram type is based on your core fears, motivations, and obstacles. You will relate to all nine types in one way or another, but your dominant type is the one that speaks the most directly to your life experience. Each type is described in full in the upcoming pages.

TYPE FOUR
·········
THE ARTIST
Sensitive
Authentic
Expressive

TYPE FIVE
·········
THE PHILOSOPHER
Cerebral
Reserved
Independent

WHAT IS THE GOAL OF THE ENNEAGRAM?

The goal of the enneagram is to help you find acceptance for who you are and freedom to become much more. Through the enneagram, you will find valid and illuminating reasons behind your unhelpful behavioral patterns. You might say "Aha! That's why I always self-sabotage my relationships" or "Oh! That's why I always lose my temper and blow up at people." This recognition and self-awareness will, hopefully, enable you to have more compassion for yourself in those circumstances. But learning about your personality's natural tendencies is not an excuse to continue in behavioral patterns that are unhelpful or harmful to you or other people. Instead, learning about these patterns is an invitation for you to get space and freedom from them...to wriggle free from the rigidity of what you have always done and find new flexibility to make new and different choices. The enneagram will help you understand why you act the way you do. The goal is that you let this empower you to stretch, take small steps out of your comfort zone, and grow into a better person than you were yesterday.

TYPE NINE

THE DIPLOMAT

Peaceful
Accepting
Friendly

TYPE EIGHT

THE WARRIOR

Confident
Strong
Assertive

TYPE SIX

THE ADVOCATE

Loyal
Cautious
Analytical

TYPE SEVEN

THE EXPLORER

Optimistic
Enthusiastic
Resilient

15

IDENTIFYING KEY OBSTACLES

Your dominant enneagram type has unique obstacles to growth that play a crucial part in the pain, suffering, or frustration you have experienced in life so far. These obstacles are patterns of thinking, feeling, or behaving that you probably developed initially as a way of coping with the world and protecting yourself. Often, these patterns of coping are no longer needed and are most likely getting in your way. For example, a child who gets scolded for crying might learn that life goes better for them if they ignore their feelings. But as they grow up, they might realize that ignoring their own feelings has caused problems, and it is a coping mechanism that they no longer need. Knowing about your unique personal obstacles to growth is crucial if you want to use the enneagram for empowerment. You must learn how you are getting in your own way if you want to get out of your own way and expand into the most confident and capable version of yourself.

IDENTIFYING KEY FEARS AND MOTIVATIONS

Your dominant enneagram type has a set of core fears and motivations that are the driving force behind your personality. While your behaviors and characteristics are what you do, your fears and motivations are the reasons why you do the things that you do. Acknowledging these fears and motivations helps you make sense of why you make the choices you make and why you see the world the way that you do. It is important that you consider these fears and motivations and the role they have played in your life. This will help you cultivate a sense of self-compassion, an essential ingredient you will need as you seek to change for the better.

"The goal of the enneagram is to help you find acceptance for who you are and freedom to become much more."

Stress type and security type

Your stress type is the number that you move toward during times of stress or insecurity. Knowing the behaviors of your stress type that you naturally fall into is a helpful way of identifying when you are under too much stress and need to find new ways of caring for yourself. But it is also helpful to know about the positive behaviors of your stress type so that you can begin to lean into these intentionally during times of stress.

Your security type is the number that you move toward during times of security and health. And as you free yourself from the unhealthy patterns or pitfalls of your dominant type, you will naturally begin to express more of the healthy behavior and character traits of your security type. It's important to note, however, that it is unhelpful and counterproductive to try to act like your security type or take on the traits of that type. Growth only happens when you accept yourself as you are, with compassion, while seeking to break free from the unhealthy or unhelpful patterns of your dominant type.

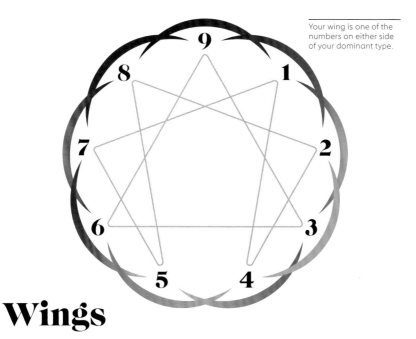

Your wing is one of the numbers on either side of your dominant type.

Wings

Your wing is either the number directly to the right or to the left of your dominant type, whichever type's traits you lean into more. For example, an enneagram type Two will either have a One wing and have several similarities to a One, or they will have a Three wing and have several similarities to a Three.

You might lean more toward one wing during the first part of life and then more toward the other wing during the second half of life. Your wing type brings nuance to your dominant type and the way you express your personality, so studying it is a helpful way to increase your self-awareness and understanding. Your wing type can also help you find more stability in your life approach, because you can access the perspectives and behaviors of your wing type when you need them as a way of finding balance and staying grounded.

Using the enneagram for empowerment

- **Take as much time as you need to identify your dominant type.** Some people take a quiz and find their type right away. Others need more time for honest self-reflection and exploration. The good news is that the path toward realizing your dominant type can be healing and growing in and of itself.

- **Read about all nine types, not just your own.** You will find helpful insight for yourself by looking through the lens of each of the nine perspectives. And with realizations about why people do the things that they do, you will expand your ability to have compassion for how other people think, feel, and behave.

- **Consider your actions.** As you learn about the enneagram, make a practice of observing your own behavior as you go about your day. Pause to ask yourself why you do the things that you do. Self-observation is important if you want to use the enneagram for empowerment.

- **Look at the full spectrum of your personality.** Don't consider just your strengths or just your weaknesses. Empowerment requires taking all of the positives and all of the negatives into account.

- **Approach your learning with humility and self-compassion.** Stay open to seeing your behavioral patterns that are hurting you or the people around you. Empowerment is about taking full responsibility for who you are—it's not about hyping yourself up. But be sure to pair this humility with self-compassion, too. Having compassion for who you are now opens up the possibility of becoming more.

A WORD OF CAUTION

- Be kind to yourself while you learn about the enneagram, because it will highlight some things about yourself that you don't like, and this might hurt. Extend the virtues of patience, understanding, and hopefulness toward yourself if you begin feeling down about yourself. All growth has growing pains.

- Focus on your own growth and empowerment. You can change yourself. But you can't change other people.

- You are unique and nuanced, and nothing can truly and fully describe you, so there will be some things about your dominant enneagram number that don't apply to you. Take with you whatever guidance is helpful and let go of the rest.

- Don't tell other people their type. This can be hurtful, because their type is based on some of their deepest fears and insecurities. They might become curious about the enneagram after seeing your own increasing empowerment. But if they want to find their own type, they will do so in their own time.

- Your enneagram type will make you feel seen and understood just as you are. This is one of the most beautiful things about it. Just be sure to differentiate for yourself who you are now versus who you want to be in the future. In other words, don't lock yourself into your personality as it is now or begin using it as an excuse to stay put in all of your current grooves and patterns. Nobody is meant to stay just as they are. We are all meant to learn, grow, and improve.

"You will relate to all nine types, but your dominant type is the one whose underlying motivations, fears, and obstacles you relate to the most."

How to find your enneagram type

1. Take the quiz on the following pages and make note of your top three scores. It's likely one of these is your dominant enneagram type, but you will need to read through the type descriptions to know for sure.

2. Read through the nine enneagram type descriptions within this chapter. As you read about each type, wait for the gut feeling that says, "This is describing what it's like to be me!" Discovering your type requires that you introduce yourself to each of the nine types and compare their life experiences to your own. Honest self-reflection is a key component of this.

3. Understand that your type is not determined by your behavior; it's determined by what goes on behind your behavior: your fears, your motivations, and your desires. You will have traits in common with other numbers. But one type will speak to the deepest parts of your life experience, and this is your dominant type.

What's your type?

This quiz is a starting point to identifying your dominant enneagram type. It will give you clues as to which type you might be, but take it with a grain of salt. After reading more about each type, you might realize you are a different type than you first expected.

Write your score next to each statement, and add up the numbers in each column. One of your top three scores is likely your dominant enneagram type.

ON A SCALE OF 0 TO 5, HOW MUCH DOES EACH STATEMENT SOUND LIKE YOU?

0 — **NOT AT ALL** LIKE ME ———— **VERY MUCH** LIKE ME **5**

1	2	3
I'm a perfectionist.	Relationships mean everything to me.	I work hard, and I'm very efficient.
I always feel like I could have done better.	I can read people and pick up on their feelings.	I can morph when I need to and fit in anywhere.
There is a right way to do things and a wrong way.	I love helping people.	I'm collected and cool.
I'm afraid that I'm not good enough.	I'm scared of being rejected or unwanted.	Failure is hard for me. I want to be impressive.
I can be harsh and critical.	Sometimes I'm overly needy or dependent.	I worry I'm a fraud or a phony.
Total	**Total**	**Total**

- [ ] I'm a romantic at heart.
- [ ] I have a creative mind.
- [ ] I'm sensitive and emotional.
- [ ] I'm often jealous or discontented.
- [ ] I'm terrified of being insignificant.

- [ ] **Total** **4**

- [ ] I do my research before trying something new.
- [ ] I like spending time alone.
- [ ] I'm often quiet and private. I only show affection to a small few.
- [ ] I hate feeling incompetent or ignorant.
- [ ] Sometimes I'm cold and unfeeling.

- [ ] **Total** **5**

- [ ] I'm intuitive and caring.
- [ ] I'm loyal and a great team player.
- [ ] I'm skeptical and don't trust easily.
- [ ] I'm scared of making the wrong choices.
- [ ] I'm more anxious than most people.

- [ ] **Total** **6**

- [ ] I'm an optimist.
- [ ] I'm spontaneous and enthusiastic.
- [ ] I love new and exciting experiences.
- [ ] I don't like thinking about painful emotions; I prefer to move on quickly.
- [ ] I can be scatterbrained and disorganized.

- [ ] **Total** **7**

- [ ] I'm tough and resilient.
- [ ] I'm confident and assertive.
- [ ] Deep down, I'm scared I'll be lied to or betrayed.
- [ ] I avoid being controlled at all costs.
- [ ] Sometimes I'm pushy and domineering.

- [ ] **8**

- [ ] I'd rather compromise than have conflict.
- [ ] I can see everybody's point of view.
- [ ] I'm easygoing and flexible.
- [ ] I hate the idea of people being mad at me.
- [ ] I'm often forgetful and unmotivated.

- [ ] **9**

"Focus on your own growth and empowerment. You can change yourself. But you can't change other people."

Getting to know the enneagram types

As you read through each of the nine type descriptions, pay attention to anything that makes you cringe or feel uncomfortable, particularly annoyed, or embarrassed. This is often a sign that you might have found your type.

Consider which type describes you best in your younger years. You have the same type your whole life, but sometimes it's more obvious when you're young and less inhibited. Reflect on what your behavior is like now, but also on what it was like back then.

You will relate to all nine types. While character traits (such as being people-oriented or assertive) might play into which type you are, remember that surface elements of your personality do not determine your type. Your dominant type is the one whose underlying motivations, fears, and obstacles you relate to the most.

Imagine how your closest friends and family members would define your biggest insecurities, shortcomings, and strengths. Getting insight from people who have known you for a long time can give you more self-awareness.

Some people find their type right away. For others, it's a longer journey that requires more self-reflection and observation. Be patient with yourself and take as much time as you need.

Type

1

THE VISIONARY

IDEALISTIC
CONSCIENTIOUS
RESPONSIBLE
DISCERNING
PURPOSEFUL
RATIONAL
PERFECTIONISTIC
ORDERLY
SELF-CONTROLLED
PRINCIPLED

Type Ones want to make themselves, other people, and the world around them better. They see the world not just for what it is, but for what it could be. And they want everything they touch to meet the highest possible standard. Seeing potential wherever they look, they are often visionaries and change-makers.

Ones tend to be conscientious rule-followers who care about having a good reputation. Their moral compass is strong, and they see the world in clear, black-and-white categories. Although Ones might sometimes be judgmental, it is important to note that they are harder on themselves than on anyone else.

A harsh voice lives in the head of every enneagram One, constantly critiquing them on what they could be doing better. Ones struggle with perfectionism and live in fear of making mistakes. Since nobody (not even Ones themselves) can live up to their standards, the key obstacle for type Ones is irritation and resentment toward themselves and other people.

What enneagram **ones** say about themselves:

"I'm responsible and reliable."

"I appreciate it when things are precise and neat."

"People can trust me to make sure things are done well."

"There's a voice in my head always talking about what I could be doing better."

"I've been called a perfectionist and told that I should 'loosen up.'"

"There's a lot of weight on my shoulders. I have a lot of responsibilities and I don't want to let anyone down."

"I make an effort to be kind and honest."

"It irritates me when people cut corners or make excuses for themselves. I get frustrated that other people don't try as hard as I do."

"I give good advice. People can trust me to have a sensible opinion."

"I'm really hard on myself and have a hard time letting things go."

"I'm good at improving things, whether that be ideas, plans, events, designs, or even grammar."

"Sometimes I come across as judgmental and harsh."

Key motivations:

To do well and be in the right.

To be respected.

To be good.

Key fears:

I will mess up.

Something is wrong with me.

I'm not good enough.

Key obstacles:

Anger and resentment

Irritation and passive-aggression

Perfectionism and control

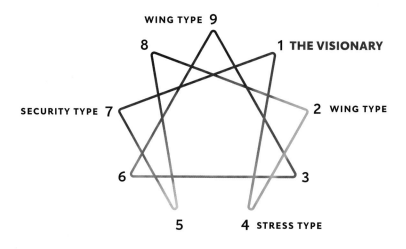

WING TYPE **9**

8

1 THE VISIONARY

SECURITY TYPE **7**

2 WING TYPE

6

3

5

4 STRESS TYPE

Wing type: 9 or 2

Your wing is either Nine or Two, whichever feels most like you. This number brings nuance and balance to how you operate and express yourself.

Stress type: 4
Security type: 7

In stress or unhealth, you take on characteristics of type Four. But in security and health, you take on characteristics of type Seven.

Considerations for growth

- **Please hear this: you were never meant to be perfect.** What you must begin to see is that things can be flawed *and* good. Things can go not as planned and exactly as they should. You can have imperfections and be perfectly acceptable just as you are.

- **Release the idea that you are in any way responsible for the behavior of other people.** Take rest in knowing that you cannot make choices for others. You can only choose how you respond to them.

- **Practice humble curiosity when you run into disagreements.** There are many points of view, and you do not always have the best one. You are not always right. This should feel like a relief, because it is what makes you human. And it gives you permission to make mistakes.

- **Cultivate kindness and understanding for yourself as you are right now.** When we feel safe and loved, we feel more freedom to grow because we're starting from a place of security and strength. So start cultivating self-acceptance now; don't save it as a reward for when you've "earned it."

- **Let go of the idea that feelings are good or bad.** To be human is to feel. Listen to your anger, because it can teach you things, and find healthy ways to express it (journaling, therapy, etc.). Anger rises up in you for a reason, and if you don't release it, it will either find its way out in hurtful ways or fester into bitterness inside of you.

Type

2

THE CONNECTOR

RELATIONAL
GENEROUS
EMPATHIC
PEOPLE-PLEASING
CHARMING
CARING
SUPPORTIVE
NURTURING
INTUITIVE
POSSESSIVE

The world of a type Two is all about relationships. They are called the connectors because building and maintaining relationships is their primary motivation. Twos have the sixth sense of empathy and can sense the needs and feelings of those around them. They are caring, supportive, and nurturing.

Friendly and charming, the endearing nature of Twos helps them make friends but often leaves them feeling depleted; it's easy for Twos to get lost in the care of other people, while neglecting their own needs. They tend to be very generous with their time, energy, ideas, and resources. But finding themselves giving more than they receive, Twos often feel taken for granted or used.

The main obstacle for type Twos is overdependence and manipulation. They care for others with the goal of being cared for in return. They love in the hopes of being loved. Driven by the fear of not being wanted and loved, type Twos overextend themselves for others so that they will feel needed.

What enneagram twos say about themselves:

"I prioritize relationships above everything."

"It's easy for me to tell what other people need. But it's hard to know what I need."

"I love helping people solve problems, make decisions, feel better after a disappointment— whatever it may be, I just love to help."

"I can sense what other people are feeling. Reading social cues is my superpower."

"In relationships, I give more than I get. I put in a lot of effort, and it's disappointing not to get the same in return."

"Being close and connected with someone is the best thing."

"I'm a great gift giver. I love finding that perfect thing."

"When someone is stressed or upset, I feel like it's my fault or my job to make them feel better."

"I have a hard time saying no, and I've been told people take advantage of me because I'm so willing to go out of my way for them."

"I love heart-to-heart conversations. Connecting on a deeper level is one of my favorite things."

"I can get so invested in helping others reach their goals that I forget about my own."

"It's important to me that I'm truly loved and needed."

Key motivations:

To have deep relationships.

To be needed and appreciated.

To be wanted and loved.

Key fears:

I will be unwanted.

I will be rejected and abandoned.

I will be alone.

Key obstacles:

Emotional denial and self-neglect

Overdependence

People-pleasing and manipulation

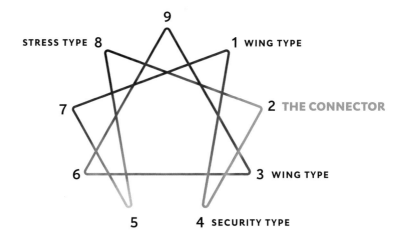

STRESS TYPE **8**

1 WING TYPE

2 THE CONNECTOR

3 WING TYPE

4 SECURITY TYPE

Wing Type: 1 or 3

Your wing type is One or Three, whichever feels most like you. This number brings nuance and balance to how you operate and express yourself.

Stress type: 8
Security type: 4

In stress or unhealth, you take on characteristics of type Eight. But in security and health, you take on characteristics of type Four.

Considerations for growth

- **Start an intentional pursuit of self-care that includes your physical, mental, and spiritual health.** The more you treat yourself like someone who is worthy of love, the more loved (and worthy of love) you will feel. And the more you care for your own needs through self-care, the more empowered you will be to love others out of a place of security and strength rather than fear and need.

- **Know that you are worthy of being loved before you offer any love.** You are free to give away your love; it is not an obligation.

- **Learn to identify and communicate your needs** (food, rest, safety, emotional support, quality time, etc.). Learn to recognize your needs and meet them intentionally, verbally asking for support as needed. Otherwise, you will resort to passive-aggressive methods of getting your needs met that end up hurting you or others in the end.

- **Find the lines between you and them.** These lines are sometimes blurred by the empathetic connection you have with others. Ask yourself: Which choices are theirs to make and which are mine? Which emotions are theirs and which are mine? Which problems are theirs and which are mine? If you feel depleted by a relationship, observe these lines. Things work better when you take responsibility for your stuff and let go of their stuff.

- **Decide what your life is about and then invite others to join you.** If you are being yourself and pursuing a life you care about, there will be people who want to share life with you. You won't need to convince anyone to stay around by proving your place in their life. You must release the idea that you have any control over whether others will stay or go. This idea will only weigh you down.

Type

3

THE LUMINARY

MOTIVATED
ADAPTABLE
IMPRESSIVE, VAIN
CONFIDENT
COMPETITIVE
PRODUCTIVE
HARDWORKING
APPEARANCE-
FOCUSED
ENERGETIC
SUCCESSFUL

Type Threes see the world through the lens of potential achievements and success. Threes set their sights high and usually accomplish what they put their minds to. Often key or popular figures in their social circles, they are called the luminaries because of their impressive and charismatic nature.

Energetic and productive, Threes are driven to succeed and willing to put in the work it takes to get there. Threes are ambitious, diligent, and determined to reach their full potential. Often, they have a gift for inspiring and helping others become their best selves, too.

Despite their apparent confidence, Threes are driven by the fear that they won't be worthy of love and acceptance. They feel they must project certain characteristics to earn a place in the world and in their relationships. The obstacles Threes face are emotional dishonesty and superficiality. In an effort to look valuable, Threes become overly competitive, put on fake appearances, and take on false traits in order to impress.

What enneagram **threes** say about themselves:

"I'm busy and efficient. I always have a running to-do list in my head."

"I can change my personality to fit in with different groups or situations."

"I keep my biggest goals and aspirations to myself. That way, if I fail, nobody will know."

"I love motivating people to be their best selves."

"I'm adaptable. Put me anywhere and I can shine...or at least fit in."

"Sometimes I miss important personal moments because I'm so focused on working toward the next thing. I know this has hurt people."

"I'm always on the lookout for what will make me more attractive, a better partner and friend, or more productive at work."

"I'm incredibly hardworking."

"I'm good at faking it, so it's hard to know if I've actually made it. I'm always worried I'll get called out as a fraud or an imposter."

"People have told me I seem insincere."

"Most of the time, I'm the most put-together and collected person in the room."

"I'm very driven to succeed in whatever I'm doing."

Key motivations:

To be successful and impressive.

To be desirable and admired.

To feel valued and worthy of love.

Key fears:

I will fail. And I will fail others.

I will be seen as phony or incompetent.

I will be worthless.

Key obstacles:

Emotional dishonesty

Superficiality

Workaholic tendencies

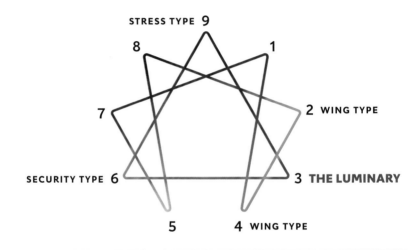

STRESS TYPE 9

8

1

7

2 WING TYPE

SECURITY TYPE 6

3 THE LUMINARY

5

4 WING TYPE

Wing Type: 2 or 4

Your wing type is either Two or Four, whichever feels most like you. This number brings nuance and balance to how you operate and express yourself.

Stress type: 9
Security type: 6

In stress or unhealth, you take on characteristics of a Nine. But in security and health, you take on characteristics of a Six.

Considerations for growth

- **Learn the importance of stillness and rest.** Intentionally take time to simply just be yourself—without your phone or electronics, without a plan or an agenda. See what happens for you in stillness; it will teach you things you need to know.

- **Expand your emotional vocabulary.** Then practice identifying and naming your own feelings and the feelings of others. It's important to slow down enough to acknowledge the feelings in and around you, and to give them space to exist with you before moving on. Emotions connect you more deeply with others. And they help you connect more deeply with who you are. A good amount of existential stress can be alleviated by identifying and acknowledging emotions.

- **Know that you are already worthy of being here and being loved.** You were put here on purpose; you don't have to earn the right to be here. Start living out of this place, where you already are worthy of acceptance and love before you accomplish a single thing. Authenticity will naturally flow out of this place, because you will have nothing left to prove.

- **Go places where you don't shine;** find your struggles and lean into them. Growth and healing happen outside of your comfort zone.

- **Figure out who you are apart from the things you are most proud of.** Who are you when you take away your most valued achievements or belongings? Who are you apart from the treasured roles you play? Find a therapist or trusted guide who can help you discover your identity apart from your success. Successes can fade or be taken away, so you want to be anchored by the pieces of you that will last.

Type

4

THE ARTIST

SENSITIVE
AUTHENTIC
EXPRESSIVE
INTROSPECTIVE
GENTLE
CREATIVE
MOODY
SELF-CONSCIOUS
EMOTIONAL
COMPASSIONATE

Fours see the world through the lens of their emotions. Sensitive, wistful, and creative, Fours desire a life that is unique and rich with meaning. With an eye for beauty, Fours are often artistic or aesthetically gifted.

Empathetic and tender-hearted, Fours have the gift of holding ambiguity and are able to find meaning in both the lighter and the darker sides of life. Fours are tuned in to their own emotions. They easily get pulled inward into the romantic and stormy world inside themselves.

Although Fours present an image of uniqueness and intrigue, they are driven by fear of not knowing who they really are. They want to have a meaningful and individual identity. They want to get enough out of life. But they worry that they are incomplete. Their key obstacles are jealousy and ingratitude: they feel that others have something they don't, and in their yearning for more, they forget to find joy in the present.

What enneagram fours say about themselves:

"I rarely see things as black and white."

"I'm good at making things beautiful and meaningful."

"It feels like I'm missing the puzzle piece in life that would make me feel settled, like I had arrived."

"I'm in touch with my emotions, I'm creative, and I have a big imagination."

"Authenticity is important. I'd much prefer someone be real with me than pretend they're perfect."

"I'm sensitive and my feelings are intense. Any single feeling can take over my whole body in a moment."

"I'm drawn toward melancholy things, like sad music or a dramatic cloudy landscape."

"I've been told I'm too dramatic."

"I romanticize everything. I can be extremely moved by a song, a movie, a conversation, or even a trip to the grocery store."

"I feel like others have reached a level of satisfaction with life that I haven't yet reached."

"I overthink how I come across to other people. I think I'm a lot more self-conscious than most."

"I feel misunderstood a lot of the time."

Key motivations:

To have a unique identity.

To live a significant life.

To be loved and understood.

Key fears:

I'm not sure who I really am.

I'm ordinary and insignificant.

I will never be loved for who I am.

Key obstacles:

Self-absorption

Emotional unrest

Jealousy and ingratitude

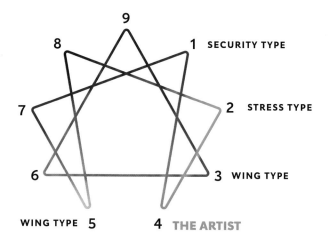

9

8   1 SECURITY TYPE

2 STRESS TYPE

7

3 WING TYPE

6

WING TYPE 5   4 THE ARTIST

Wing Type: 3 or 5

Your wing type is either Three or Five, whichever feels most like you. This number brings nuance and balance to how you operate and express yourself.

Stress type: 2
Security type: 1

In stress or unhealth, you take on characteristics of a Two. But in security and health, you take on characteristics of a One.

Considerations for growth

- **Know that you are not missing something.** You are already a whole and complete person, just as you are. And your uniqueness is irrefutable. What will you do, now that you have already arrived in wholeness and completeness?

- **Observe yourself and ask: Am I investing my time and energy into my thought-life or into my real life?** The more you act like the kind of person you want to be, the more you will feel sure of who you are. It's okay that you withdraw into your own world to process things. But make sure you come back out and actively participate in shaping your own life, because the actions you take today create your future.

- **Don't give emotions more power than they have.** Emotions are important, but they are ultimately just something you experience. They are not you. Emotions tell the truth about how you're feeling, but they don't always tell the truth about reality. They don't have the power to read anyone's mind or motives, and they can't see as many sides to a situation as you can. You are bigger than your emotions.

- **Know that while you are beautifully complex and unique, you are not an anomaly.** You belong here. You fit in here. You are here on this earth (right where you are, just as you are) because you were meant to be here.

- **Realize that fulfillment and contentment will only happen for you in the present.** There is no person or thing in the future that will bring it to you. It is not on the road ahead. Contentment is an inside job: you will need to find it for yourself. But be sure to reach out for support in your pursuit.

Type

5

THE PHILOSOPHER

CEREBRAL
OBJECTIVE
SELF-SUFFICIENT
RATIONAL
PRIVATE
COMPETENT
DISCIPLINED
RESERVED
INDEPENDENT
THOUGHTFUL

Fives see the world in terms of information. As keen observers of life, Fives have the ability to collect, sort, and store lots of information and ideas. Fives are rational, disciplined, and consistent.

Type Fives live in their heads: they approach life thoughtfully and analytically and are unlikely to be swayed by emotion. They enjoy alone time more than any other enneagram type. Their social energy is limited; when it comes to group activities, they often prefer to observe rather than participate. But their dependable and intentional nature makes them devoted partners and friends.

Fives are driven by the fear of not having enough: not having enough knowledge to be competent, not having enough energy for relationships, and not having enough dexterity to get through life successfully on their own. This means their key obstacle is stinginess. In fear of not having enough, they hold on tightly to what they do have: information, resources, energy, and even love and affection.

What enneagram fives say about themselves:

"It doesn't bother me to be alone."

"I'm independent and self-reliant. And I admire these traits in others."

"In groups, I tend to sit back and observe rather than be the life of the party."

"I'm curious and love learning everything there is to know about a subject."

"I never feel like I'm enough for people. People need more from me than I have to offer."

"I'm objective and reasonable; I don't get carried away with emotions."

"I'm in my head a lot of the time; I think through things before I act."

"I've been told I'm condescending and insensitive."

"I'm a private person; I don't like sharing personal details about my life."

"I've been called a wallflower, an introvert, and a lone wolf."

"I've often felt like I'm on the outside looking in."

"I'm good at being thrifty and frugal."

Key motivations:

To be capable and competent.

To be self-reliant and autonomous.

To know enough and have enough.

Key fears:

I will be inadequate and incompetent.

My privacy will be invaded.

I won't have enough (energy, love to offer, resources, etc.).

Key obstacles:

Stinginess and selfishness

Timidity

Mindset of lack

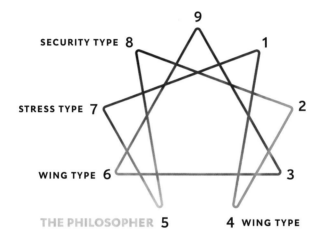

SECURITY TYPE **8**

STRESS TYPE **7**

WING TYPE **6**

THE PHILOSOPHER **5**

9

1

2

3

4 WING TYPE

Wing Type: 4 or 6

Your wing type is either Four or Six, whichever feels most like you. This number brings nuance and balance to how you operate and express yourself.

Stress type: 7
Security type: 8

In stress or unhealth, you take on characteristics of a Seven. But in security and health, you take on characteristics of an Eight.

Considerations for growth

- **Remember that thoughts cannot create the life you want to live.** Only you can do that. Your action creates your life. When you find yourself living in your head, come down into your body, and make some tangible movements and choices that bring your hopes and ideas to life. The words you say, the art you create, the places you travel, the person your arms wrap around, the causes you give to—these are the things that create your life.

- **Know that you are so much more than your thoughts and your opinions.** No matter how much you do know or don't know, you are loved and treasured for so much more.

- **Notice when you find yourself obsessively collecting facts, insights, or objects.** Sometimes when you compulsively collect, you're trying to fill up an emptiness inside of you. But your heart will not fill up by consuming things alone: a full heart comes from giving things away. You must give away your love, effort, and energy in order to feel full.

- **Please hear this: you already know enough to live your life successfully.** Confidence and ability develop by doing things, not by thinking things. If you want to learn how to surf, you have to get out in the water and try standing up on a surfboard. And then you have to try, fail, and keep trying. You are not expected to know how to do things before you start doing them. Your confidence and abilities in life will grow through practice, not by knowledge.

- **You were made with a heart that can experience love so that you can experience love.** Relationships do not have to overwhelm you or ask too much of you. Learn how to ask for the boundaries you need.

Type **6**

THE ADVOCATE

PASSIONATE
CAUTIOUS
LOYAL
STRATEGIC
CARING
INTUITIVE
ANXIOUS
DEPENDABLE
DEVOTED
SKEPTICAL

Sixes see the world in terms of security and threat. Carefully choosing where they put their trust, their main motivation is to feel supported and secure. But Sixes look out for the safety of others, too, offering loyal and steadfast support to the people and the causes that they care about. They are caring and dependable.

Sixes are team players. More than any other enneagram type, they have their eye out for the common good, always wanting a solution that's best for everyone. They typically spend plenty of time playing devil's advocate or troubleshooting before making decisions. Sixes are passionate about the issues they care about. And they are devoted advocates for the people, institutions, and values they stand for.

Driven by a fear that they won't have the security or the guidance they need, the key obstacle for Sixes is anxiety and self-doubt. They are vigilant and skeptical, often in their heads analyzing and planning future events. This leads to a thought-life that is full of what-ifs, worst-case scenarios, and worry.

What enneagram  sixes say about themselves:

"I'm a caring person and a steadfast friend."

"I feel stressed and anxious a lot of the time...a lot more than most people."

"I'm very loyal to people. If you're my friend, you can bet that I'll stick up for you and give you second chances."

"I want whatever's best for everyone. I'm a great team player."

"I worry about the future."

"I take things seriously and I'm a deep person."

"Troubleshooting is second nature to me, and I often play the devil's advocate."

"Decisions are hard for me. I'm always worried I'll make the wrong choice."

"I'm 100% dedicated to the causes I commit to."

"People have told me I need to 'take a chill pill' and not worry so much."

"It's hard for me to turn my brain off and just relax."

"I'm very passionate about the people and beliefs I care about."

Key motivations:

To be safe and secure.

To have guidance and support.

To feel calm and to choose the right path.

Key fears:

I will be scared and unsure.

I will put my trust in the wrong place.

I will make the wrong choices.

Key obstacles:

Worry and anxiety

Self-doubt

Negative outlook

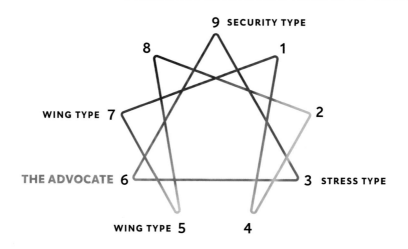

9 SECURITY TYPE

8

1

WING TYPE 7

2

THE ADVOCATE 6

3 STRESS TYPE

WING TYPE 5

4

Wing Type: 5 or 7

Your wing type is either Five or Seven, whichever feels most like you. This number brings nuance and balance to how you operate and express yourself.

Stress type: 3
Security type: 9

In stress or unhealth, you take on characteristics of a Three. But in security and health, you take on characteristics of a Nine.

Considerations for growth

- **Start developing self-trust.** Sometimes, when you wish you were braver, what you actually need is to trust yourself more. Remember the times you've leapt and landed on your feet. Celebrate the times you've made a choice that was a good one. Make note of the times you felt scared, but still made it through. Make small promises to yourself (like, "I will drink one glass of water this morning") and then do everything in your power to keep those promises. This will help you build self-trust, so that instead of asking yourself, "Am I brave enough to leap?" you can tell yourself, "I can trust myself to land."

- **Make room for ambiguity in your life.** Not all questions have answers. And most decisions have more than one right option. But that's okay. What's important is that you're living the kind of life you want to live along the way.

- **Know that even if it's uncomfortable, it's okay to have worried thoughts.** You are bigger and more powerful than your thoughts, even when they feel overwhelming. When worried thoughts come to your mind, take a few steps back and just observe them for what they are. Because you are not your thoughts. You are you. And your thoughts are just something you experience.

- **Find the people in your life who will ask you good questions**, not give you more answers.

- **Find activities that help you come down out of your mind and into your body.** A lifetime of experience is ingrained in you. But you must start paying attention to your body, your senses, and your feelings in order to get in touch with that confidence and wisdom.

Type 7

THE EXPLORER

OPTIMISTIC
ENTHUSIASTIC
IMPULSIVE
ADVENTUROUS
INDULGENT
SPONTANEOUS
POSITIVE
ASSERTIVE
PLAYFUL
RESILIENT

Type Sevens see life through a filter of optimism and positivity. They find the bright side of everything. Sevens move through life like explorers—full of curiosity and wonder, always on the lookout for their next exciting discovery or pursuit. And Sevens know how to have fun; they thrive on spontaneity and adventurous experiences.

Imaginative and bold, Sevens have the assertiveness it takes to instigate new ideas and get things started, and they want to pack in as much fun as possible along the way. Sevens love having stories to tell about their insights or experiences. Their optimism and playfulness makes them incredibly resilient.

The key obstacle for Sevens is emotional avoidance. Driven by fear of feeling empty, lonely, or overwhelmed by sadness, Sevens avoid acknowledging the more negative and uncomfortable emotions in life. Instead, they fill themselves up with entertainment and distractions. This impulsive avoidance of negative emotions leads to overindulgence and a dismissal of other people's feelings and needs.

What enneagram sevens say about themselves:

"I'm an optimist. I can always find a silver lining."

"I like to keep life fun and interesting. Sometimes this makes me impulsive."

"I'm always on the move, but I never feel like I'm doing enough."

"I can make quick decisions, but sometimes I'm too rash and hasty."

"Even in the midst of a trial or crisis, I know how to lighten the mood and cheer people up."

"I hate being bored. And if things get boring, I'm the one to mix things up."

"Spontaneity and freedom are important to me."

"When things go wrong, I move on quickly. It's better to keep looking ahead rather than wallow in sadness."

"Sometimes I frustrate people by doing a rushed or haphazard job."

"I'm always on the lookout for my next adventure or opportunity."

"I've been called shallow, flaky, and goofy. But I just like to keep things lighthearted."

"It's hard for me to stay organized."

Key motivations:

To feel satisfied and content.

To avoid pain and suffering.

To be taken care of.

Key fears:

I will feel empty or unhappy.

Sadness will overwhelm me if I let it.

I won't feel safe and stable.

Key Obstacles:

Emotional avoidance

Impulsivity

Overindulgence

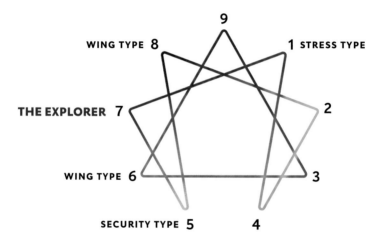

Wing Type: 6 or 8

Your wing type is either Six or Eight, whichever feels most like you. This number brings nuance and balance to how you operate and express yourself.

Stress type: 1
Security type: 5

In stress or unhealth, you take on characteristics of a One. But in security and health, you take on characteristics of a Five.

Considerations for growth

- **When an uncomfortable feeling comes up that you'd rather ignore, pause and sit with it for a few minutes.** Emotions are sometimes painful, but they are always temporary, even the worst ones. So let yourself feel them. Because if you ignore your feelings, they will follow you around. But if you acknowledge them and accept them for what they are, you will feel free as you journey on.

- **Let the present moment fill you up.** Use all five senses to practice observing the rich details of the here and now.

- **Learn to be present with pain.** When someone shares how they are struggling, refrain from trying to cheer them up or fix their problem. Instead, ask questions: "Can you tell me more about that?" And reflect back to them what they're saying: "You feel really disappointed right now." They will feel cared for, and you will learn that you are strong enough to move through pain instead of sidestepping it.

- **When you can't stop consuming (food, experiences, distractions, etc.), ask yourself what void you are trying to fill.** If you can't stop reading about other people's lives, there might be pain in your own story you're trying to avoid. When you can't stop eating comfort food, you might have an emotion that needs to be comforted. Ask yourself what hunger you are really trying to feed.

- **When it comes to the negatives in life, start saying "and" instead of "but."** Instead of saying, "Yes, that thing happened but it's fine," try saying "Yes, that thing hurt a lot and I know I will be okay."

Type

8

THE WARRIOR

CONFIDENT
PASSIONATE
STRONG
DECISIVE
CONTROLLING
PROTECTIVE
INDEPENDENT
ENERGETIC
OPPOSITIONAL
HONEST

Type Eights move through the world with power and a keen awareness of the power around them. They sense who is in control versus who is being controlled, who has the power versus who is more vulnerable, and who is fair and just versus who is taking advantage of the weak. Eights want to know who's in charge, and often, it's them.

Confident and strong, Eights thrive on intensity and take life head-on with energy and charisma. They passionately stand up for what they believe in and passionately protect the people they care about. They value honesty and justice above all else. They want to experience life to the fullest, so they struggle with excessiveness: doing too much, saying too much, and consuming too much.

Despite their toughness, Eights have tender hearts and are scared of being hurt or betrayed. The key obstacles for Eights are excessiveness and an issue with control. Fueled by a fear of being hurt or controlled, Eights put up a tough exterior, ignore their more tender feelings, and attempt to control the environment and the people around them.

What enneagram **eights** say about themselves:

"I'm resilient and tough. You can't break me."

"Independence is important to me. I hate feeling controlled, and I don't like being told what to do."

"I get really protective with the people I care about."

"I have a gut instinct about things, and I can make decisions quickly."

"Honesty is important. I can handle the truth—just give it to me straight."

"I'm efficient, productive, and assertive—taking initiative is no problem for me."

"I feel like I'm too much for people."

"Sometimes I take over situations or steamroll other people's opinions and feelings."

"I'm intense—my highs are high and my lows are low. I love with a passion; I hate with a passion."

"I've been called bossy, pushy, and aggressive."

"I stick up for people. And it really hurts when others don't stick up for me."

"I often feel misunderstood."

Key motivations:

To protect self and others from harm and control.

To maintain independence.

To have justice.

Key fears:

I will look weak and vulnerable.

I will be taken advantage of and betrayed.

I will be treated unfairly.

Key obstacles:

Control issues

Vulnerability avoidance

Excessiveness and overexertion

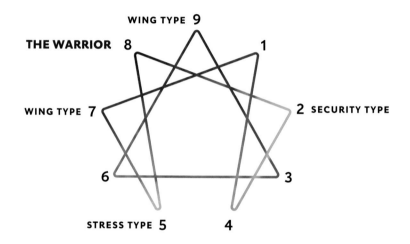

WING TYPE **9**

THE WARRIOR **8**

1

WING TYPE **7**

2 SECURITY TYPE

6

3

STRESS TYPE **5**

4

Wing Type: 7 or 9

Your wing is either Seven or Nine, whichever feels most like you. This number brings nuance and balance to how you operate and express yourself.

Stress type: 5
Security type: 2

In stress or unhealth, you take on characteristics of a Five. But in security and health, you take on characteristics of a Two.

Considerations for growth

- **Notice each time you find yourself trying to change what is not yours to change, or trying to make a decision that is not yours to make.** You cannot decide what another person will feel or do, whether they will stay or go, or how they will live their life. This is not up to you. Let this realization release the weight off your shoulders. Because you are only in control of you. And you are only responsible for your actions.

- **Reconnect with your own tenderness.** Do things that bring out your softer side, like spending time with animals or revisiting nostalgic hobbies or places from your childhood. Reconnect with your own gentleness.

- **Before you act, pause, soften, and take a breath.** Consider what the response to your actions will be. No matter how justified you feel, the actions you think you should take won't always get you the results you want.

- **Know that you are strong enough to feel the feelings behind your anger and passion.** Without acknowledging your more vulnerable emotions, you will miss out on the depth and intensity of life and relationships that you desire. What gets expressed as anger is often something else. Ask yourself: What feeling is behind my anger?

- **Realize that no matter how much energy and resilience you have, your body is not invincible.** Learn to give your body rest and care. It needs it.

Type

9

THE DIPLOMAT

PEACEFUL
FLEXIBLE
ACCEPTING
FRIENDLY
APPROACHABLE
FORGETFUL
KIND
INDECISIVE
ADAPTABLE
COMPLACENT

Nines see the world in light of the peacefulness or instability of their connections and relationships. They are sensitive to any kind of discord and want everyone to get along. Flexible and adaptable, they value having a calm environment and will usually sacrifice their own preferences and feelings to keep it that way.

Typically, Nines are approachable and friendly, loved by many and disliked by few. They have a unique ability to see things from a thousand different points of view. While they are accepting and inclusive, they are also frequently indecisive and forgetful of their own opinions and needs.

In fear of losing their connections and relationships, Nines often lose themselves. Their key obstacle is self-ignorance and passivity. Absorbed in their pursuit of keeping harmony, Nines easily morph into versions of the people around them, adopting their preferences and priorities, and losing sight of who they really are. This lack of individuality and differentiation ends up causing them more existential crisis and anxiety in the end.

What enneagram **nines** say about themselves:

"I'm easy to get along with."

"Peace and kindness are important to me. I would rather compromise than have a fight."

"I wish I was more ambitious, but I typically don't have much drive."

"Making decisions is hard for me. It's easier just to base them on what the people around me want."

"I'm a good listener, and I can understand a lot of different perspectives."

"I feel like nobody really cares about my opinions or needs."

"People find me comforting and calming. But inside, I feel stressed and anxious a lot of the time."

"I will go out of my way to keep people happy with me or to keep a relationship stable."

"I'm generally accepting and want everyone to feel valued and included."

"It's easy for me to become like the people I spend time with. I quickly adapt to new routines or become convinced of new opinions."

"I like having a cozy space. It's important that my environment is comfortable and calm."

"I wish I had more discipline and motivation."

Key motivations:

To maintain relationships.

To avoid conflict and discomfort.

To have inner peace of mind.

Key fears:

I will lose my relationships.

I will create discord or stress.

I don't really matter.

Key obstacles:

Fatigue and lethargy

Emotional numbness

Passivity and self-ignorance

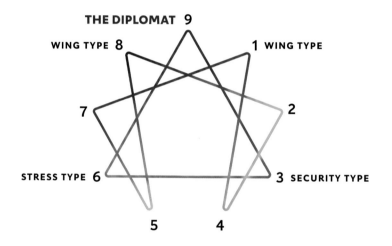

THE DIPLOMAT 9
WING TYPE 8
1 WING TYPE
7
2
STRESS TYPE 6
3 SECURITY TYPE
5
4

Wing Type: 8 or 1

Your wing type is either Eight or One, whichever feels most like you. This number brings nuance and balance to how you operate and express yourself.

Stress type: 6
Security type: 3

In stress or unhealth, you take on characteristics of a Six. But in security and health, you take on characteristics of a Three.

Considerations for growth

- **Take notice whenever you quiet your opinion to avoid disagreement**, stuff your feelings down to avoid upsetting someone, or ignore your gut instinct in order to avoid causing stress. Recognize that this is a passive way of controlling the energy in a relationship or a group.

- **Know that healthy relationships between two people have space for two people.** Half the space in every relationship you are in is completely your space to fill. This space is for your presence, your goals, your thoughts and ideas, your feelings, your input, and your needs and desires. Trusting and healthy relationships can accommodate differences.

- **Take time to get to know you.** You are naturally good at connecting harmoniously with others. But it's important, for your own mental health, that you figure out what makes you, you (and not them). Start digging into important questions about your identity: What are your deepest goals? What do you value most? What are your strengths? And what do you want to make out of your life?

- **Know that you matter.** You do make an impact. Your voice is wanted. You are here on purpose for a purpose.

- **Realize that feeling at peace is an inside job.** If you want to feel at peace, you will have to actively work through your anxiety. Stable relationships and cozy spaces are comforting for a time, but they are only Band-Aids. If you are anxious on the inside, no amount of peace in the environment will give you inner peace. If you want to feel at peace, you must actively pursue this. Be sure to reach out to a therapist or a trusted guide for support.

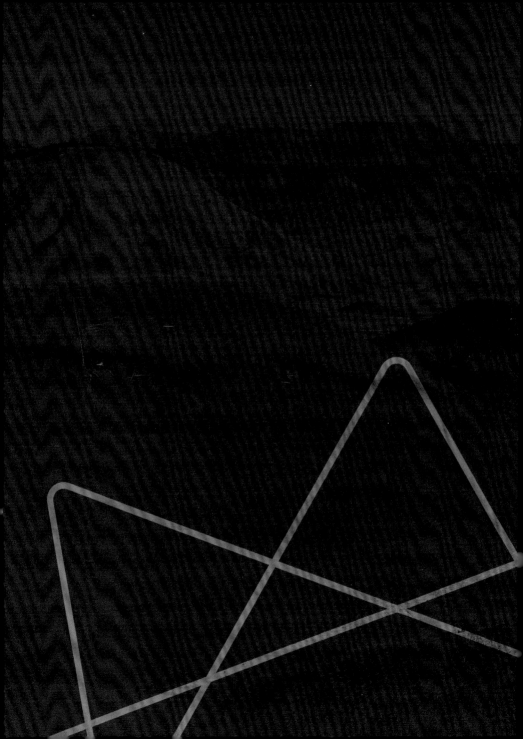

The Enneagram & Self-Empowerment

Live out your strengths, cultivate self-compassion, and discover the behaviors that are holding you back.

Start with self-compassion

When you want to change for the better (which is what the enneagram is all about), it's natural to be hard on yourself for having weaknesses that hold you back. But if you want to make any sort of positive life change, what you need to do is soften your attitude toward yourself. What you need to do is to start with self-compassion.

Your enneagram number doesn't only show you your patterns of behavior that are holding you back; it also shows you the pain that drives that behavior. It's important to look at this pain with warmth and self-compassion, so that you can find freedom from the pain that is trapping you into those loops of unhelpful behavior. Self-compassion is not about making excuses for yourself. (It's important that you take full responsibility for all of your own thoughts, feelings, and choices.) Self-compassion is about regarding yourself with warmth and understanding, regardless of what changes you would like to see in yourself.

The benefits of self-compassion are numerous. According to Dr. Kristin Neff, a pioneer in the field of self-compassion research, self-compassion increases a person's happiness, life satisfaction, motivation, relationships, resilience, physical health, and ability to cope with stressful events. It makes sense, then, that self-compassion would empower you to make healthy changes in your life. Self-compassion is the environment in which new good things can grow.

Self-compassion is the environment in which new good things can grow.

If your best friend made a mistake, would it be helpful for you to criticize them and increase their guilt? To scold them for not having more self-control and self-awareness? Or would it be more helpful if you said this: "I know you are trying to do better. You're not the only one who is struggling. You are human, and we all struggle. Tomorrow is a new day, and you can try again. I still love you. This mistake doesn't define you." As you learn about your enneagram number and seek to change for the better, remember to be a friend to yourself. Celebrate your strengths, your values, and your hopes. Extend warmth and understanding to yourself while you work on your weaknesses. See yourself as the whole and complex person that you are, doing your best.

You are only human, so it is only fitting that you see yourself with humor and laugh with yourself. You have flaws and quirks and inconsistencies just like everyone else. And you should always take ownership of your own choices, thoughts, and feelings. But don't ignore the pain and the fears that go along with them. These things are a part of you, too, and they need your compassion in order to heal. Start with self-compassion, and you will set the stage for growth and change.

Respond mindfully to stress

There will always be reasons for you to experience stress (physically, emotionally, spiritually, relationally, or otherwise) because some amount of fear, suffering, or frustration will always exist in the world around you.

There will be events that occur outside of your control; you cannot control how other people live their lives any more than you can control the weather. While you can't change the fact that reasons to stress will always exist, you can identify what commonly triggers stress for you and learn to respond to that stress mindfully, instead of reacting to it in ways that are unhelpful to you and to your relationships.

TYPE	WHEN YOU ARE TRIGGERED BY:	NOTICE YOUR TENDENCY TOWARD:
1	Imperfection or messing up	Criticism (toward self or others)
2	Rejection (real or perceived)	Manipulation, possessiveness
3	Failure (or fear of failure)	Self-deceit, emotional denial
4	Lack of significance or identity	Jealousy, ingratitude
5	Scarcity (of physical or emotional resources)	Hoarding, greed
6	Threat of danger or insecurity	Hypervigilance, negative outlook
7	Boredom	Overindulgence, hastiness
8	Feelings of weakness or powerlessness	Excessiveness, control
9	Relational disconnection	Self-numbing, people-pleasing

STRATEGIES FOR STRESS

- Acknowledge your emotions.
- Do something nice for yourself.
- Take a hot shower.
- Journal about your emotions.
- Go for a walk.
- Talk to someone about your pain or fear.
- Notice what your body is feeling.
- Take deeper breaths.
- Eat a healthful meal.
- Get a good sleep.
- Remind yourself that it's okay to feel stressed sometimes.
- Drink a glass of water.
- Spend time in nature.
- Give yourself a hug.

Live out your strengths

Your strengths are the positive character traits that feel like second nature to you. Think of strengths as the things you are good at without even having to try. What comes naturally to you at work but seems difficult to other people? Which of your attributes would your friends lovingly say they are jealous of? What would the people who have known you the longest (or the deepest) say that you're good at? These are your strengths.

Using your strengths on a regular basis is key to empowerment because doing things you are good at reinforces your feeling of "I am capable," which is the basis of confidence. Using your strengths gives you a lot of life satisfaction, too, because there's a strong sense of purpose that comes from putting your strengths to work. Using your natural strengths gives you tangible evidence that your contribution to the world and your presence in the world are important and unique.

"The good life," wrote Martin Seligman, the founder of positive psychology, "is using your signature strengths every day to produce authentic happiness and abundant gratification." To use your strengths, you must first identify what your strengths are.

On the following page are common strengths that people with your enneagram type often share. Some of them might apply strongly to you, and some not so much. These will get your wheels turning as you start discovering what your natural strengths are. Then it's time to put your strengths to work! Find ways to use them in your daily life, and you will feel your inward sense of confidence and empowerment begin to grow. When you use your strengths, you feel powerful, and you feel like *you*.

1 VISION PRUDENCE JUSTICE SELF-CONTROL INTEGRITY ORGANIZATION INNOVATION FOCUS	SOCIAL INTELLIGENCE KINDNESS GENEROSITY EMPATHY HUMOR TEAMWORK NURTURING COMPASSION	PERSEVERANCE ADAPTABILITY LEADERSHIP SELF-CONTROL EFFICIENCY SOCIAL INTELLIGENCE ENCOURAGEMENT COMPETENCY
SENSITIVITY KINDNESS CREATIVITY OPENNESS PURPOSE VULNERABILITY COMPASSION APPRECIATION OF BEAUTY	CURIOSITY LOVE OF LEARNING PRUDENCE OBSERVATION DISCIPLINE REFLECTION LOGIC COMPOSURE	PLANNING INTUITION LOYALTY SINCERITY PREPARATION HUMILITY COLLABORATION THOUGHTFULNESS
ENTHUSIASM GRATITUDE BRAVERY AWE CURIOSITY OPTIMISM CREATIVITY HUMOR	BRAVERY ADVOCACY LEADERSHIP INTENTIONALITY DETERMINATION CONFIDENCE HONESTY RESILIENCE	PERSPECTIVE DIPLOMACY ACCEPTANCE UNDERSTANDING KINDNESS EMPATHY LISTENING PATIENCE

"Using your natural strengths gives you tangible evidence that your contribution to the world and your presence in the world are important and unique."

Questions for reflection

———

What were your strengths
as a child and a teenager? Do you
still see those strengths within
yourself?

•••

What would your closest friends
say you are good at?

•••

What hobbies, routines, or pursuits
would allow you to use your
strengths daily?

Empowered thinking

No matter how rational a person you are, you will still have some negative thoughts that are simply irrational. And that's okay. Thoughts are only thoughts; you are bigger than your thoughts and have the power to observe which are true and which are not.

But consider how one irrational negative thought, if it feels like a true thought, can disempower you: the thought "they don't like me" brings emotional pain along with it (such as sadness or anxiety), which triggers an impulse to make regrettable choices (such as overindulgence or perfectionism) in reaction to that pain. All enneagram types fall into patterns of negative thinking, but cultivating awareness of these patterns will help you break free of them and develop patterns of empowered thinking instead.

Empowered thinking is the ability to recognize these negative thinking traps—these irrational or false thoughts that trap you in a cycle of negative emotions and unempowered behavior. Negative thinking traps are also known as cognitive distortions, which form the basis for Cognitive Behavioral Therapy, developed primarily by Aaron T. Beck and Dr. David D. Burns. Twelve different kinds of negative thinking traps are defined on the following pages. You will probably recognize all of them! But depending on your enneagram type, you will most likely gravitate toward certain ones.

While learning to observe your thoughts and recognize these negative thinking traps, it's important to reflect on the deepest fears of your enneagram type that drive so many of your thoughts. Noticing the fear behind your thoughts will help you treat yourself with compassion, a necessary element for positive growth.

NEGATIVE THINKING TRAP

IRRATIONAL NEGATIVE THOUGHT

EMOTIONAL SUFFERING

UNEMPOWERED CHOICES

EMPOWERED THINKING

1. Notice and observe the irrational negative thought objectively, without judgment.

2. Recognize the fear behind it with self-compassion.

3. Add an alternative empowered thought for hope or for grounding.

4. Take a step back from your thoughts and choose empowered behavior.

Negative thinking traps

ALL OR NOTHING
You see things as either good or bad; there is no middle ground.

MENTAL FILTER
You filter out the positives and focus on the negatives, or vice versa.

OVERGENERALIZATION
You think that if one bad thing happens it means more bad things will happen.

PERSONALIZATION
You think other people's behaviors are about you.

CATASTROPHIZING
You magnify a problem or shortcoming and think worst-case scenarios are the most plausible outcomes.

MIND READING
You assume you can tell what others are thinking.

MINIMIZATION

You make your wins smaller than they are and exaggerate your failures.

FORTUNE TELLING

You believe you can predict a negative future outcome.

LABELING

You attach a broad label to yourself or someone else because of one event or action.

"SHOULD" STATEMENTS

You treat your own expectations as though they are set in stone or universal standards.

EMOTIONAL REASONING

You treat your feelings as factual evidence.

DISQUALIFYING THE POSITIVE

You reject or argue against your positive experiences.

(These definitions are adapted from *Feeling Good: The New Mood Therapy* by Dr. David. D. Burns.)

EMPOWERED THINKING

MOTIVATING FEARS	I will mess up. I'm not good enough. Something is wrong with me.

NEGATIVE THINKING EXAMPLE	**ALTERNATIVE EMPOWERED THOUGHT**
The essay would have been perfect, but it had a silly typo in it. Now it's totally ruined. *(All or Nothing)*	The essay had a flaw in it, like everything does, but most of it was great! I will see it for what it is: flawed but good.
I should eat healthier. *("Should" Statements)*	I haven't made it a priority to eat healthy, but I can choose to now if I want to. Either way, it's my choice.
I should know better by now. I'm such a failure. *(Labeling)*	Failing does not make me a failure. It just makes me human. This mistake is here to teach me something; I will learn from it and grow.

EMPOWERED THINKING

TYPE 2

MOTIVATING FEARS	I will be unwanted. I will be rejected and abandoned. I will be alone.

NEGATIVE THINKING EXAMPLE	ALTERNATIVE EMPOWERED THOUGHT
They have a frown on their face. They must be mad at me. I must have made them angry. *(Personalization)*	They have a frown on their face. They might be tired, or sad, or mad at someone else or at themselves.
They made that negative remark about me last week that hurt my feelings. It's all I can think about. *(Mental Filter)*	They made a hurtful remark about me. But they have also made several positive remarks about me. I will think about these positive remarks, too.
They still haven't found a job. I bet they feel scared. Maybe they'd appreciate some job-hunting ideas. *(Mind Reading)*	They still haven't found a job. I know how I would feel in that place, but I don't know how they feel. I will let them tell me how they feel and what they need.

EMPOWERED THINKING

TYPE 3

MOTIVATING FEARS	I will fail. And I will fail them.
	I will be seen as phony or incompetent.
	I will be worthless.

NEGATIVE THINKING EXAMPLE	ALTERNATIVE EMPOWERED THOUGHT
Yes, I did get that promotion. But honestly it's probably a fluke—they just needed to find someone for that position quickly. *(Disqualifying the Positive)*	Yes, I did get that promotion. I have worked really hard at this company, and my hard work is paying off. They could have chosen someone else, but they chose me.
I ran five miles. But so what? I have friends who run marathons. *(Minimization)*	There are a lot of people who can't run five miles, and some people who can run a marathon. Regardless of what other people can or can't do, it is very meaningful for me to run five miles. I'm excited and proud of myself!
I should put more time into self-care. *("Should" Statements)*	Nobody is in charge of how much self-care I "should" or "shouldn't" do. Self-care is something I haven't prioritized lately, but I can prioritize it now if I want to and if I choose to.

EMPOWERED THINKING

TYPE 4

MOTIVATING FEARS	I'm not sure who I really am. I'm ordinary and insignificant. I will never be loved for who I am.

NEGATIVE THINKING EXAMPLE	ALTERNATIVE EMPOWERED THOUGHT
I feel so jealous lately. They must have feelings for someone else. Why else would I feel this way? *(Emotional Reasoning)*	I feel jealous. But I know that jealousy is just a feeling; it's not a fact. I will take the facts of the situation into consideration.
I made a big mistake at work. My boss is going to be so mad. I'll probably get called in, and I might even get fired! That would look so bad on my resume. *(Catastrophizing)*	I made a mistake at work. But I'm human, and humans make mistakes. So I'm hopeful that my boss will be understanding. This is more likely than me getting fired.
I would never say that unless I was super angry. They must be angry. *(Mind Reading)*	What they said sounded angry to me, but I cannot read minds. I will have to ask them what they meant if I want to find out.

EMPOWERED THINKING

TYPE 5

MOTIVATING FEARS	I will be inadequate and incompetent. My privacy will be invaded. I won't have enough (energy, love to offer, resources, etc.).

NEGATIVE THINKING EXAMPLE	ALTERNATIVE EMPOWERED THOUGHT
I tried mini-golf once and it was a horrible experience. I'm not making that mistake again. *(Fortune Telling)*	I've had one bad experience with mini-golf. But this does not mean that all future experiences with mini-golf will be negative. I don't know the future. It is possible that I could have a positive experience playing mini-golf.
I can't believe I didn't know the answer to that question. I'm so dumb. *(Labeling)*	Not knowing the answer to a question doesn't make me dumb. It just means I'm human. And I happen to be a human who's really smart about a lot of things!
I know this is the correct opinion. Anything else is just stupid. *(All or Nothing)*	I feel sure about my opinion. But I'm only human; I am not all-knowing. I will stay receptive to learning more because I know there's a possibility that I am wrong.

EMPOWERED THINKING

MOTIVATING FEARS

I will be scared and unsure.
I will put my trust in the wrong place.
I will make the wrong choices.

NEGATIVE THINKING EXAMPLE	ALTERNATIVE EMPOWERED THOUGHT
That turned out to be a good decision for me. But that could have just been luck. *(Disqualifying the Positive)*	It turns out that I made a good decision. I weighed my options and made a good choice!
It was a good first date, except for the fact that I got nervous and asked the same question twice. They probably thought I wasn't listening to them and just didn't care! There's no way they're going out with me again. *(Catastrophizing)*	I was nervous and asked the same question twice. They might have been annoyed by it, or they might have thought it was funny or cute. Regardless, most of the date went really well, so this one detail will most likely be insignificant.
I ate there one time and got sick because the fish had gone bad! You just can't trust seafood restaurants. *(Overgeneralization)*	One seafood restaurant serving expired fish does not mean that all seafood restaurants serve expired fish. This is like saying that just because one book I read was boring, all books are boring.

EMPOWERED THINKING

MOTIVATING FEARS	I will feel empty or unhappy. Sadness will overwhelm me if I let it. I won't feel safe and okay.

NEGATIVE THINKING EXAMPLE	ALTERNATIVE EMPOWERED THOUGHT
I don't see the red flags about this person that my friends see. All I can see is the good stuff! (Mental Filter)	I see many positive traits in this person. And I also see some negative traits. Both of these things are important to consider.
I have a really good feeling about it, so I don't think I need to be worried. (Emotional Reasoning)	I feel optimistic about this. But this is a feeling. There are also facts that I should take into consideration and give equal value.
Sure, I feel sad if I think about it. But this is so small in the big scheme of things! There's so much of life to be enjoyed. (Minimization)	In the near future, I will go back to enjoying life. But at this moment, I feel very sad. This is a big deal to me. And this moment is important.

EMPOWERED THINKING

TYPE 8

MOTIVATING FEARS	I will look weak and vulnerable. I will be taken advantage of and betrayed. I will be treated unfairly.

NEGATIVE THINKING EXAMPLE	ALTERNATIVE EMPOWERED THOUGHT
They didn't speak up to defend me in that argument. Clearly they don't care about me at all. *(All or Nothing)*	Verbally arguing on my behalf versus not caring about me are not the only two options here. They might have wanted to help but not have known how to. There are lots of possibilities.
I don't like vegetables! I hate salads, and I had to eat steamed broccoli all the time as a kid and hated it. *(Overgeneralization)*	I don't like steamed broccoli or salads. But there could be other vegetables prepared other ways that I would like.
My friend went behind my back and totally betrayed me. You can't trust anyone. You can't rely on anyone but yourself. *(Mental Filter)*	It hurts to be betrayed. But I actually have more people in my life who are loyal and loving to me then who are not. I know that there are good people worth noting.

EMPOWERED THINKING

TYPE 9

MOTIVATING FEARS	
	I will lose my relationships.
	I will create discord or stress.
	I don't really matter.

NEGATIVE THINKING EXAMPLE	ALTERNATIVE EMPOWERED THOUGHT
I just don't feel like there's anything wrong with doing it. *(Emotional Reasoning)*	I don't feel strongly about this issue. But I will honor my mind in this matter, too, and think through all of the consequences rather than going with what I feel.
They seem annoyed. They must be annoyed with me. *(Personalization)*	There's a possibility that they could be annoyed with me, but it could just as likely be something else. People get annoyed for all sorts of reasons. It's also possible that they are just tired or hungry.
I don't know anything about that subject. I'm so stupid. *(Labeling)*	I'm not informed about that subject. But not knowing something doesn't make me dumb. There are other things that I am informed about.

Empowering questions

1. How will I choose to define "good enough" right now?

2. What is mine to do and what is theirs to do?

3. What is it like to be me right now?

4. What are the feelings and what are the facts?

5. Am I open to changing my mind?

6. What are some possible positive outcomes?

7. What do I feel in this moment?

8. Can I pause and sit with this for a while before moving forward?

9. What is my priority here?

Live by your values

Your values are what you consider to be the most important things in life: your deepest beliefs about how you think you should live. They are things like authenticity, family, hope, advocacy, and creativity.

Your values are what make life meaningful and worthwhile. Living in step with your values gives you confidence that you are on the right path. But living against your values brings guilt and self-doubt, because betraying one of your values means that you are betraying one of the deepest parts of who you are.

For example, if family is one of your deepest values, but you devote all of your free time to personal pursuits, this will create dissonance in your soul. If you are prioritizing one of your values (personal achievements), another one of your values (family) is getting ignored. Imagine if you began consistently prioritizing family during at least half of your free time. You would know that you were living authentically and honestly, because your actions would embody something you believe is of the utmost importance in life. When your actions match your values, you have confidence that you are on the right path.

It's important to know what your values are so that you can know whether or not you're on the right path. This concept is a key component of Acceptance and Commitment Therapy, a therapeutic approach that helps individuals overcome mental health obstacles and create a life that feels worth living, which was developed by the clinical psychologist Dr. Steven Hayes. Can you name some of your own values? If not, bring to mind some of your role models and consider which character attributes make them inspiring to you. Ask yourself what kind of legacy you want to leave behind. For example, is it more important that people say you were innovative, honest, adventurous, or compassionate? The answers to these questions will give you clues as to what you value most.

VALUES SET YOUR COMPASS.

They point you in the direction you want your life to move in.

**DISTRESS
SELF-DOUBT**

**PEACE
CONFIDENCE
EMPOWERMENT**

← →

**Ignoring or violating
your values**
(my actions and behaviors
do not match my values)

**Living in step with
your values**
(my actions and behaviors
match my values)

Living by your values helps you:

- Make good decisions

- Set authentic goals

- Know how to prioritize your
daily life

- Increase your self-assuredness

- Feel satisfied and purposeful

Questions
to consider

———

Am I being true to what I value?

•••

Do my beliefs and my behaviors
match up, or is there a disconnect
between what I think is important
and what I prioritize?

•••

What activities could I begin
practicing that would allow me
to live out my values on a
regular basis?

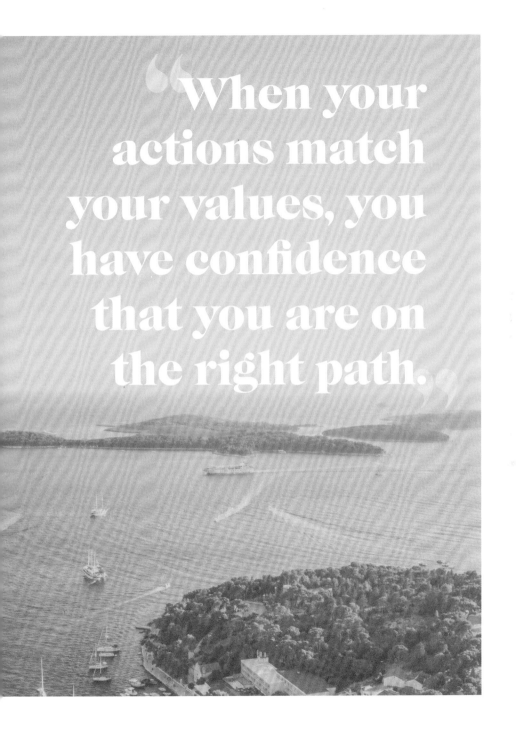

"When your actions match your values, you have confidence that you are on the right path."

THE CONNECTOR

COMPASSION
RELATIONSHIPS
GENEROSITY · SERVICE
INTIMACY · EMPATHY
THOUGHTFULNESS

Example of Compassion and Service: Taking care of your own needs as you would the needs of others.

THE VISIONARY

INTEGRITY
SELF-CONTROL
KINDNESS · FAIRNESS
GOODNESS · JUSTICE
IMPROVEMENT

Example of Kindness: Choosing to be kind instead of critical.

THE LUMINARY

AUTHENTICITY
GROWTH · PRODUCTIVITY
HOPE · CONFIDENCE
AMBITION · INTEGRITY

Example of Authenticity: Expressing your true feelings, even when admiration or acceptance is at risk.

Common core values

Consider which common core values of your enneagram type most resonate with you. Then take inventory of the other virtues, strengths, and aspects of life that you most deeply value.

THE ARTIST

SELF-EXPRESSION
INDIVIDUALITY · MEANING
ORIGINALITY · HONESTY
SIGNIFICANCE · BEAUTY

Example of Self-Expression: Prioritizing time to be creative.

THE PHILOSOPHER

AUTONOMY
UNDERSTANDING
SKILLFULNESS · LEARNING
TRUTHFULNESS · KNOWLEDGE
INDEPENDENCE

Example of Learning:
Investing time and/or
finances into education.

THE ADVOCATE

COMMUNITY
LOYALTY · SUPPORT
FAITHFULNESS · COURAGE
TRUSTWORTHINESS
COLLABORATION

Example of Loyalty: Speaking
up for the people and things
that you care about, even
when it's scary.

THE EXPLORER

JOY · FREEDOM
INNOVATION · OPTIMISM
FRIENDSHIP · EXPLORATION
ADVENTURE

Example of Friendship:
Being vulnerable enough to
experience real friendship.

THE DIPLOMAT

CONNECTION · PEACE
UNITY · ACCEPTANCE
INCLUSIVITY · KINDNESS

Example of Connection:
Reaching out to form new
connections and initiate
new friendships.

THE WARRIOR

FREEDOM · PASSION
BOLDNESS · JUSTICE
HONESTY · ADVOCACY
RESPECT

Example of Advocacy:
Prioritizing time to support a
cause you believe in.

Self-care for each type

Self-care is the choice to be kind to yourself. You know what it means to be kind to others— to be friendly, gentle, appreciative, patient, understanding, empathetic, encouraging, and caring. Extending this attitude and approach of kindness toward yourself is really all that self-care is about.

You can make this choice to be kind to yourself at any given moment, during any given day. And this choice will look different based on what you need in that present moment. The kind choice might be to acknowledge one of your own accomplishments, or it could be to eat an energizing breakfast, to make time for something that's important to you, to go to sleep on time, to advocate for yourself, to exercise, to stay true to your values, to take a break, to drink enough water, or to speak words of compassion and understanding to yourself during emotional suffering.

As a child, at least to some extent, you were taken care of—you were given food and naps and water, you were told to eat vegetables, you were comforted, and you were given things to help you grow, like education and encouragement. Now that you are grown up, it is your job to take care of yourself. This can be a fun and enjoyable responsibility if you make it one, because the goal of self-care is to bring more peace and vitality into your life.

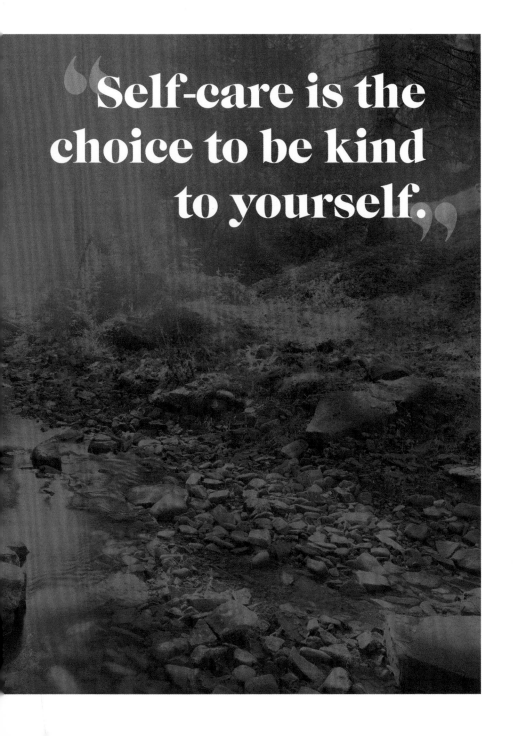

"Self-care is the choice to be kind to yourself."

Self-care

 Heart

- Watch a comedy show, read a funny book, or call the friend who always makes you laugh.

- Play games that you enjoyed as a child.

- When you feel frustrated with yourself, speak to yourself as if you were speaking to a friend, if they were in your shoes. Say these things out loud to yourself in the mirror, or write them down on a piece of paper, so that they have more poignancy.

 Body

- Start seeing food on a spectrum of less nutritious to more nutritious, instead of in categories of healthy or unhealthy. French fries don't have many vitamins or minerals to offer, so they're lower on the spectrum than some things. But everything in life is a balance. Just be sure you're getting foods that are high on the spectrum, too, like vegetables, nuts and seeds, and other whole foods.

- Find a way to exercise that feels fun and maybe even a little goofy, like roller-skating, hula-hooping, playing Frisbee, taking a dance class, rock climbing, or joining a soccer league.

 Mind

- Take three long, deep breaths through your nose.

- When you want to say "should" or "should have," say "could" or "could have" instead.

- Make a list of concerns that are your responsibility to take care of versus ones that are not your responsibility.

- Every time you critique yourself, pay yourself one genuine compliment, too.

Self-care

 Heart

- Practice giving to those who cannot give in return; for example, volunteer to play with animals at a local shelter.

- Ask yourself, "If a friend of mine was experiencing what I'm experiencing right now, what would they need?" And then give yourself that thing.

- When listening to someone talk about their stress or feelings, imagine having a beautiful vase sitting beside you. Visualize their feelings flowing into that vase, instead of letting them seep into you.

 Body

- Give yourself a hug. Crossing your own arms over opposite sides of your body is soothing and comforting.

- View exercise as an act of kindness to your body. Your body wants to move so that it can feel healthy and strong. Use exercise as a gift to your body just as it is now (not to try to change it), and you will grow your sense of body- and self-acceptance.

- When you feel emotional discomfort or anxiety start sweeping in, ask your body where it's holding or feeling that emotion. Then, place your hand firmly on that place and take a few minutes to close your eyes and breathe deeply.

 Mind

- Find a new hobby or activity to pursue on your own— one just for your own enjoyment and enrichment.

- Take yourself out to eat. Take yourself out on dates. Notice what it feels like to be with yourself.

- Keep a simple emotion journal: notice when you feel sad or uncomfortable, and pause to write down the time of day, the feelings you're experiencing, and any connected thoughts and events.

Self-care

 Heart

- Plant a flower garden. Keep bird feeders full in your yard. Care for things that are nonproductive in return.

- Use crayons or finger paints to draw a picture representing how you feel inside.

- Gather nail polishes, jewels, glitter, and nail stickers, and give yourself an artistic manicure. Get creative and let your imagination lead the way.

 Body

- When you eat, turn off your phone and electronics. Chew slowly, putting your fork down between bites. Practice savoring every taste and texture.

- Take long, hot showers and baths.

- Use exercise as a way to get in touch with your body and to ground yourself in the present. Pay attention to what your feet feel each time they touch the earth. Listen to your breath, feel your lungs and heartbeat, and observe each muscle that contracts to help you move.

 Mind

- Allow spans of silence to exist in conversations before you respond. Practice pausing and taking deep breaths while you're listening to others.

- Take "pause" days. Do only things that are nonproductive and don't have an obligation attached. Ask yourself, "What do I feel like doing at this moment? What would fill up my soul?"

- Choose one emotion to contemplate each week, and observe when and how it shows up in your life (e.g., embarrassed, disappointed, jealous).

Self-care

 Heart

- Find a creative outlet that serves others and draws your focus outward.

- Make a gratitude collage with photos, magazine cut-outs, textiles, or other materials.

- Find a box or locket to hold your feelings when you're not able to. When big feelings sweep in but your attention is needed elsewhere, you can acknowledge the feelings for what they are, then visualize placing them in the box.

 Body

- Learn about the emotionally healing benefits of food. For example, cashews are high in a calming amino acid called tryptophan. Use food to honor your emotions instead of trying to change them.

- Smile at strangers. Hug your loved ones. Keep your gaze lifted.

- Drink water often and find a delicious way to eat (or drink) lots of greens. Water and green foods are cleansing.

 Mind

- Take quick gratitude breaks. For three minutes, write down everything you can think of that you're grateful for or happy about.

- Go outside often to look up at the sky and around at the world. Feel your perspective open up. Feel your chest loosen.

- For every feeling you name, name one fact of reality, too.

Self-care

 Heart

- Volunteer your time to a cause you care about.

- Write a letter of gratitude to someone who has positively impacted you.

- Make a tissue paper collage: bring to mind an emotion you'd rather avoid, and contemplate it while you cut pieces of colorful paper into shapes and use glue to arrange them on paper.

 Body

- When you eat, give gratitude for all the people and nature sources that worked to get it to you—from the farm or the field, all the way to your plate. Let food be a reminder of your interconnectedness with the world and of how well you are cared for.

- Establish intentional rhythms of engaging with the world and then stepping away for solitude and rest, instead of waiting for energy depletion to scare or surprise you.

- Spend time outside connecting with nature. Notice what all of your senses are experiencing as you move through it, and breathe it in.

 Mind

- Speak words to yourself that encourage a mindset of abundance: "I have enough, I am enough."

- Splurge on little things for your own enjoyment or benefit.

- Learn a new skill (social, physical, or otherwise), and embrace the process of stumbling and finding your balance. This process itself will help you grow confidence and capability.

Self-care

 Heart

- Go stargazing, climb to the top of something high and admire the view, or go somewhere new to watch the sun rise or set. Cultivate a sense of awe.

- Cross your arms over your chest and give yourself a big squeeze.

- Create a playlist full of songs that represent all the different emotions you've experienced in the past month. Add some songs that represent the feelings you'd like to experience more often.

 Body

- When you eat, after you eat, and later in the day, ask yourself: How does this food make me feel emotionally and physically?

- Use exercise as a way to release nervous energy from your body, and then ground yourself in the calming energy of the present.

- Do a five-minute body check-in. From your feet to your head, notice what each part of your body is feeling in and around it—the breath going in and out of your nose, the weight of your eyelids, your heartbeat, your breath.

 Mind

- Keep a self-trust journal. Write down the good choices you've made, even the tiny ones. Write down the promises you make and keep, the goals you meet, and the routines you stick to.

- Practice taking small emotional risks to increase your comfort with discomfort. Eat a food you've never tried before, or tell an embarrassing story at a party. Remember that courage is cultivated.

- For every negative outcome you predict, brainstorm two possible positive outcomes.

Self-care

TYPE 7

 Heart

- Find a meditative hobby that will allow you to keep busy with your hands, like weaving, knitting, gardening, coloring, or throwing pottery.

- Have an interpretive dance party in your room: turn on a song that matches your current emotions and then start moving your body as if you were acting out the feelings.

- Watch a movie that represents a painful feeling in your life right now.

 Body

- Pay attention to all five of your senses and what they're experiencing in the present moment.

- Use exercise as a way of finding rest: let it release you from the busyness of your mind and pull you down into the gravity of your body.

- Find new and exciting ways to eat fruits and vegetables. Go on an exploration for the most delicious or interesting toppings. Your health doesn't have to be separate from the fun part of your life.

Mind

- Practice being by yourself in quietness, without distractions or entertainment. Start in small increments if this is difficult for you.

- Learn the details behind the everyday miracles in your life and reflect on them throughout the day. Practice observing the details, and you will gradually find it easier to be content in the present.

- Print out a list of emotion words and keep it handy to help you name and acknowledge your true emotions throughout the day.

Self-care

 Heart

- Remind yourself of goodness and innocence. Spend time playing with animals or the children in your life. Find pictures of yourself as a child and keep them around your home.

- Look at your emotions with curiosity and gentleness instead of judgment. Let them be what they are and teach you what they will.

- Gather craft supplies and create a collage. Bring to mind an emotional issue you would rather avoid; visualize it there with you and hold it in your heart as you create your collage.

 Body

- Find an enjoyable high-intensity exercise that provides a good release for your aggression and excess energy, like boxing, high-intensity interval training, or rock climbing.

- Place your hand firmly on your heart while closing your eyes and breathing deeply.

- Instead of restricting certain foods and feeling restrained, simply challenge yourself to eat more nutrient-dense foods.

 Mind

- Practice sharing more of your vulnerable emotions with those who are closest to you, and ask for help getting your emotional needs met.

- Speak the mantra: "I release the false idea that I have control over the people or world around me. I am free to make my own choices, but that is all."

- Set a timer for five minutes, grab a scratch piece of paper, and unload your brain, writing down everything and anything that comes to your mind.

Self-care

TYPE 9

 Heart

- Volunteer your time. Remember that the things you do (and don't do) actually make a difference.

- Go for an emotion-walk. Bring one painful feeling or issue to mind, and take a walk around the block with it. Visualize yourself holding space for it and letting it be what it is while you walk.

- Plant a vegetable garden or even just a few potted vegetables outside your door. Give away what you grow to friends or to those in need.

 Body

- Keep nourishing, whole foods around that you enjoy but that allow for spontaneity: berries, nuts, seeds, fruit, hard-boiled eggs, etc. Healthy food doesn't need to be fancy or well-planned.

- Drink plenty of water and smoothies made with fresh fruit or greens. These will help you feel more focused, more alert, and more alive to your own experience.

- Move every day. Whether you do yoga, ride your bike, do ten jumping jacks in your living room, or climb a mountain, just make sure you move. Remember that exercise gives you way more energy than it takes.

 Mind

- Write down your top three to five priorities in life and keep the list somewhere visible. Revisit it every few weeks to see if it needs to be changed.

- Practice saying "no, thank you" instead of saying "sorry, but..."

- Verbalize your preferences, even simple ones, or the ones you feel very flexible about.

Self-care affirmations

1. May I allow myself to be imperfect.

2. May I care for myself lovingly.

3. May I feel sure of my value.

4. May I feel sure that I belong here.

5. May I be generous with myself.

6. May I expect good things for myself.

7. May I feel at ease in the present moment.

8. May I be gentle with myself.

9. May I make room for my own feelings and thoughts.

The Enneagram and Relational Empowerment

Honor the differences between you and others, find the commonalities you share, and learn to navigate relationships well.

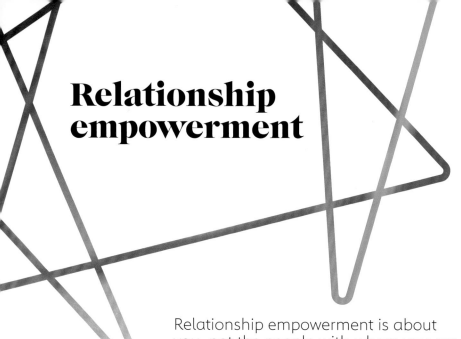

Relationship empowerment

Relationship empowerment is about you, not the people with whom you are in relationships. Since you cannot change or improve other people (you can only change and improve yourself), this section of the book is all about you becoming more empowered to navigate your relationships well.

THE ENNEAGRAM CAN HELP YOU:

- Find the commonalities between you and another.

- Honor the differences between you and another.

- Open your perspective.

- Increase your compassion and understanding.

- Learn to communicate more effectively.

- Identify and express your needs.

- Discover how to keep healthier boundaries.

SUBTYPES, STANCES, AND CENTERS OF WISDOM

The following three sections will teach three facets of the enneagram that deepen our understanding of ourselves and others: stances, subtypes, and centers of wisdom. These aspects of the enneagram will give you personalized insights into your needs in relationships, your communication and processing style, and your steps for healthy boundary setting.

Not everyone experiences the world the same way you do. Learning about the enneagram is like learning that there are nine basic types of eyeglasses and each one shows the world with a different set of colors, a different set of textures, and a different set of things that are in and out of focus. Once you realize that other people (like your mom, your friend, your coworker, your spouse, etc.) are all wearing different types of eyeglasses than you are wearing, relationship dynamics start to make a lot more sense. You start to understand why other people act and react the way that they do and why it is so different from how you might act and react.

The three subtypes

For each enneagram type, there are three subtypes, or versions, of that type, which represent different priorities and needs: the social subtype, the sexual subtype, and the self-preservation subtype. Any enneagram type can be any subtype, and this subtype will influence how they express their personality.

Social subtype	Sexual subtype	Self-preservation subtype
THESE TYPES PRIORITIZE THE NEED FOR **GROUP BELONGING** AND **SOCIAL STATUS**.	THESE TYPES PRIORITIZE THE NEED FOR **MEANINGFUL INDIVIDUAL CONNECTIONS** AND **EXPERIENCES**.	THESE TYPES PRIORITIZE THE NEED FOR **SECURITY** AND **MATERIAL NECESSITIES**.

All of us have physical needs, social needs, and a need for deep connection and meaning. And each of these needs is important. But we each naturally focus our attention on some of these needs more than the others, allowing the others to fall out of focus. Sometimes it's confusing or off-putting when other people don't share the same priorities that we do, but learning about subtypes will bring some clarity to those situations. You will understand that you naturally just focus on different needs than other people do. In relationships, you have to tell other people what your needs are. And you have to ask them what their needs are, too, if you want to know.

Your subtype has to do with which needs you instinctively prioritize in life, and which factors or issues you most naturally pay attention to. Consider these scenarios:

When you walk into a party, what do you pay attention to first?

1. The group dynamics and social structure at play: who's there, who's hosting, who's with who, if notable people are there, etc.

2. A connection you'd like to make—with a person, an opportunity, or an experience—that would make your evening meaningful and exciting.

3. The material details of the situation: the food and drink options, the budget you guess was spent on the event, and the fire exits.

When you make a big life decision, which outcome are you more naturally inclined toward?

1. The outcome that ensures good social support, a good reputation, or community.

2. The outcome that gives you a life experience that feels meaningful and important to you.

3. The outcome that maintains your financial security and makes the most logistical sense.

When you invest in a new living room sofa, which of the following will be your priority?

1. The sofa that will look the most impressive and/or be best suited to your social hosting needs.

2. The sofa that is the most beautiful to you and/or the most special and unique.

3. The sofa that's the best deal and/or the comfiest to sit on.

In general, a social subtype is more likely to choose answer 1 in each of these scenarios. A sexual subtype is more likely to choose answer 2. And a self-preservation subtype is more likely to choose answer 3.

SOCIAL PRIORITIES SUBTYPE

Social subtypes prioritize group belonging. Their attention is drawn toward things like community, group dynamics, social structure, roles, and recognition. They are driven by a need to feel like they have a place in society or in a community. They often consider things like membership, citizenship, reputation, status, or the needs of the team.

SEXUAL PRIORITIES SUBTYPE

Sexual subtypes prioritize one-to-one connections. Their attention is drawn toward interpersonal bonding, meaningful attraction, and satisfaction. They are driven by a need to feel deeply connected with and authentically attracted to other people as well as various facets of their life, such as their beliefs, their career, their hobbies, or their pursuits. They often consider the details of what will give them a viscerally meaningful experience.

SELF-PRESERVATION PRIORITIES SUBTYPE

Self-preservation subtypes prioritize physical needs. Their attention is drawn toward things like safety, security, and material comfort. They are driven by a need to feel physically taken care of and at ease. They often consider things like financial security, food and hygiene, preparations, health, preventative measures, and creature comforts.

Any type can have any subtype. For example, you can be an enneagram One with a social subtype, an enneagram One with a sexual subtype, or an enneagram One with a self-preservation subtype, and so on. Regardless of your dominant enneagram type, your subtype adds a layer of depth to the explanation of your personality. Although a Four will always look different than a Six, a Four and a Six who share a subtype will experience more things in common than they would if they had different subtypes. Your dominant type describes the key elements of what makes you tick, while your subtype describes what you prioritize and pay most attention to in life.

"In relationships, you have to tell other people what your needs are. And you have to ask them what their needs are, too, if you want to know."

Subtypes and relationships

- **Contemplate your subtype and which needs in life you naturally prioritize:** needs for social interaction, needs for intimacy and purpose, or needs for material security and comfort. These are all important needs. Start noticing which needs you naturally pay more attention to in daily life versus which ones others do. This will help you make sense of why you approach situations and solve problems differently than other people do.

- **An important need is propping up each thing you prioritize in your life.** And the same goes for the people with whom you have relationships. The need to feel calm and secure props up the priorities of keeping a routine, making your bed every morning, brushing your teeth every night, or wearing clothes that feel comfortable on your skin. The need for social belonging props up the priority of spending time with friends or connecting with people on social media. Disagreement occurs when priorities clash—for example, when you want to go to the restaurant that will provide a more unique and connective experience but they want to go to the restaurant that fits everyone's budget. Once you see disagreements in light of each person's needs, it will help you navigate those disagreements with more compassion and understanding, for them and for yourself.

- **In conflict, learn to express your point of view in terms of your needs rather than the other person's problem.** For example, instead of saying, "It's not okay for you to go around telling everyone my business," you can say, "I want to feel comfortable being open and vulnerable with you. So I need to know that you will keep personal details about my life private." Taking ownership of your own needs will empower you to be strong during conflict, while avoiding a defensive approach or an attacking one.

- **Validate the importance of your own needs and the needs of others.** The need to be financially secure, the need for social involvement, and the need for intimacy and meaning are all important needs.

- **You have a natural inclination toward prioritizing some needs over others.** But sometimes it is fitting to set aside one need in order to make room for one that is more helpful relationally. For example, you might find yourself pursuing someone romantically not because you authentically like them, but because of their status. The need for social belonging that drives this behavior is a valid need. But you can set it aside, in this instance, and prioritize your need for authenticity and emotional connection instead—if you choose to. In other words, instead of operating on autopilot, you can bring awareness to which need you are trying to fulfill and then mindfully decide whether you should prioritize that one or a different one.

- **What you naturally pay attention to might be very different from what your friend, your boss, or your partner most naturally pays attention to.** In a committed partnership, one person might pay most attention to the other person's safety: if their car is in working order, if they are saving well for retirement, and if they are getting medical checkups once a year. Meanwhile, the other person might pay most attention to what will maintain the intimacy in the relationship, like emotional check-ins and romantic gestures. Having this awareness teaches you the importance of expressing your needs, rather than assuming that others will naturally intuit them. For example, instead of feeling frustrated that your partner never initiates social activities, you could express, "I love our one-on-one time, but sometimes I want to spend time with groups of people, too, because it's important for me to feel connected socially."

"Once you see disagreements in light of each person's needs, it will help you navigate those disagreements with more compassion and understanding, for others and for yourself."

- **Arguments often arise from a clash of priorities and needs.** But if everyone's needs are acknowledged, then you can de-escalate the conflict and begin to negotiate with the goal of everyone's needs being met. So when you feel angry, pause to ask yourself: What need do I have that's not being met here? And what need might they have that is not being met here? A child's tantrum can often be avoided by making sure their needs are met, like getting enough sleep, enough food, and enough acknowledgment of their emotions. Grownups are pretty much the same way. We need rest, we need food, we need comfort, we need connection. Resolution often begins with verbally recognizing needs and then finding ways together to meet those needs.

- **Ask others open-ended questions about their priorities and needs:**

  » Will you tell me more about what is so meaningful to you about keeping the house clean?

  » I'd love to hear about why it is important for you that we do social things on the weekends.

  » I know you really care about keeping things in our relationship new and exciting; can you tell me more about that?

The three stances

Your enneagram stance describes your interpersonal style and typical pattern of getting your needs met. Think of your stance as the direction of movement that comes most naturally to you as you move through life finding ways to meet your own needs...needs such as security, freedom, or connection.

Compliant stance	Withdrawn stance	Assertive stance
TYPES 1-2-6 MOVE TOWARD OTHERS	TYPES 4-5-9 MOVE AWAY FROM OTHERS	TYPES 3-7-8 MOVE AGAINST OTHERS

Those in the **compliant stance** (types 1, 2, and 6) move toward others to get their needs met. Ones move toward others for approval, Twos for love, and Sixes for security.

Those in the **withdrawn stance** (types 4, 5, and 9) move away from others to get their needs met. Turning inward, Fours move away from the sense that they lack something in the outside world, Fives from the feeling that they are inadequate, and Nines from conflict and discomfort.

Those in the **assertive stance** (types 3, 7, and 8) move straight ahead, and often *against* others, to get their needs met. Threes move toward their goals, Sevens toward satisfaction, and Eights toward their own agenda.

Learning about your enneagram stance will bring unique insight into your own tendencies regarding healthy boundaries (or lack thereof) in relationships. Healthy boundary-keeping is empowering for everyone. But in order to keep healthy boundaries, you must first learn what boundaries are, how to assert them, and how to respect them.

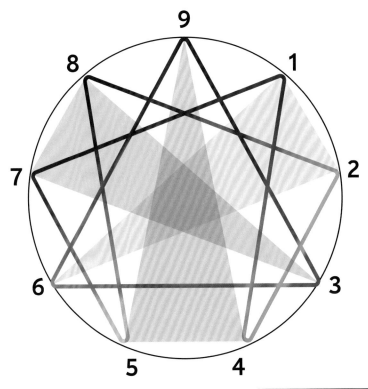

Types in the compliant stance struggle to identify boundaries. Types in the withdrawn stance struggle to assert boundaries. And types in the assertive stance struggle to respect boundaries.

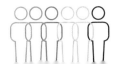

What are boundaries?

Boundaries are the lines between you and other people. When you keep healthy boundaries, you take ownership of and responsibility for your own emotions, thoughts, and behaviors, while letting others take responsibility for theirs. Accepting and respecting these lines paves the way for relationships where each person feels respected and cared for.

Your stuff	Their stuff
YOUR EMOTIONS	THEIR EMOTIONS
YOUR THOUGHTS	THEIR THOUGHTS
YOUR PROBLEMS	THEIR PROBLEMS
YOUR GOALS	THEIR GOALS
YOUR NEEDS	THEIR NEEDS
YOUR PREFERENCES	THEIR PREFERENCES
YOUR FEARS	THEIR FEARS
YOUR PAIN	THEIR PAIN
YOUR DECISIONS	THEIR DECISIONS
YOUR CHOICES	THEIR CHOICES
YOUR BELIEFS	THEIR BELIEFS
YOUR FEELINGS	THEIR FEELINGS
YOUR BODY	THEIR BODY
YOUR LIFE	THEIR LIFE

Note that boundaries might look different for children and some differently abled adults. This is a broad overview of the meaning of boundaries, and there are many nuances depending on the type of relationship you are in.

POOR BOUNDARIES MIGHT LEAD TO:

- Relationship burnout.

- Resentment.

- Feeling overly dependent on others for emotional stability.

- Feeling depleted by a sense of obligation to love others instead of feeling uplifted by the opportunity to love others.

- Suffering unnecessarily from emotions or stress that are not your own.

- Regarding others as less capable or independent than yourself by forcing your help, protection, or opinion onto them.

- Frustrating others by blaming them for your emotions and expecting them to mind-read your needs.

- Hurting those closest to you by expending too much energy on people who are not your priority.

- A myriad of other issues.

MUTUAL HEALTHY BOUNDARIES LEAD TO:

- Relationships in which you can celebrate the connection you have over shared emotions, beliefs, experiences, and desires.

- The ability to peacefully navigate the differences and disagreements that exist between yourself and others.

What can you control?

You have a lot of power in your relationships. However, all of it has to do with how you choose to conduct yourself, because this is what lies within your realm of power. You can choose what you decide to do with the feelings you experience. You can choose how to treat others. You can choose how to live your life.

However, you cannot control other people. This is not in your power. You cannot make their choices for them, and you cannot change their thoughts, their feelings, or their behavior.

This is why it's so important to recognize boundaries. We cause ourselves and each other a lot of pain and frustration when we try to change or control what we don't have (and shouldn't have) the power to change or control.

IN RELATIONSHIPS

You can:

- Make requests.
- Offer help.
- Share your emotions.
- Express your thoughts and opinions.
- Assert your boundaries.
- Offer love and invest in connection.

You can also:

- Say yes or no to requests.
- Accept or refuse help.
- Decide how to respond to their emotions.
- Choose how to respond to their thoughts and opinions.
- Respect or disregard their boundaries.
- Accept or pull back from offers of love and connection.

But you cannot:

- Control their emotions.
- Control their thoughts.
- Control their behavior.

You also cannot:

- Change their emotions.
- Change their thoughts.
- Change their behavior.

In relationships (even in the closest ones) you ultimately cannot change or control how someone else will feel or what they will choose to do. This is not in your power. Likewise, they cannot change or control how you will feel or what you will choose to do. This is not in their power. You can each only choose how you behave toward one another. So it's important to take ownership of and responsibility for what is yours. And it's just as important to not take ownership of or responsibility for what is not yours.

The compliant stance

TYPE 1
THE VISIONARY

TYPE 2
THE CONNECTOR

TYPE 6
THE ADVOCATE

These types may or may not be extroverted. But when it comes to getting their key needs met, they turn toward other people. Ones turn toward others in search of approval and affirmation of their goodness, Twos turn toward others in search of love and affection, and Sixes turn toward others in search of security and stability.

These types have a strong sense of obligation to meet the needs or expectations of other people. They often feel so committed to doing the "right thing" in relationships, the "loving" thing, or the "team player" thing, that they struggle to see the boundaries between themselves and others. As a result, they often feel exhausted by relationships or taken for granted, but have difficulty explaining why. Because of their difficulty seeing or admitting their own needs, they sometimes resort to passive-aggressive behavior as a way to get those needs met.

STARTING POINTS FOR HEALTHY BOUNDARIES

- **Practice identifying the boundary lines between you and other people.** Pause to ask yourself: Is this my emotion or their emotion? Is this my choice or their choice? Is this my responsibility or their responsibility?

- If you are feeling exhausted by a relationship, **consider which personal boundaries you have accidentally crossed.** You might be carrying a load that does not belong to you, solving a problem that is not yours to solve, or filling a need that is not yours to fill.

- **Anytime the word "should" pops up, look into its validity.** Often, when you say "I should," that "should" is actually based on someone else's expectations. Remember that you get to create your own standards, set your own expectations, and follow your own convictions and beliefs.

- **Practice taking ownership of your own emotions and needs.** If you feel hurt and you'd like that to be acknowledged, you can say, "I feel hurt and I'd like to talk about why." If you feel insecure in your relationship and you'd like to talk about it, you can say, "I feel insecure in our relationship and I'd like to talk about it." Waiting for someone to notice your emotions and needs, giving the silent treatment, or giving subtle cues only leads to frustration for everyone. Your emotions are yours, and if you'd like them to be acknowledged, it is your responsibility to say something.

- Before you go out of your way for someone, take a few minutes to consider why you are doing it and how you feel about doing it. **Remember that gifts given out of resentment are not true gifts.** Love given with the motive to receive love in return is not true love. And favors paid out of obligation are often signposts of poor boundaries.

The withdrawn stance

TYPE 4
THE ARTIST

TYPE 5
THE PHILOSOPHER

TYPE 9
THE DIPLOMAT

These types tend to keep to themselves more than others do and often feel overwhelmed by the world around them. Some of them are very social and relational. But when it comes to meeting their essential needs, instead of looking outward or toward other people for fulfillment, they turn inward and withdraw from others.

Fours retreat inward, withdrawing from the sense that they lack something in the outside world. Fives retreat inward, withdrawing from the feeling that they are inadequate in the outside world. And Nines retreat inward, withdrawing from the discomfort and conflict in the outside world. These types feel their boundaries deeply; they want to have enough of their own space and the freedom to make their own choices. But they have trouble articulating and asserting their own boundaries, and as a result they often feel that their boundaries are being pushed or disrespected.

STARTING POINTS FOR HEALTHY BOUNDARIES

- **Realize that your needs and preferences must be stated in specific and concrete language** if you want them to be acknowledged and respected.

- **When you say "yes" without wanting to say "yes," contemplate why.** Fours often have trouble saying no because they don't want to be disliked, Nines because they don't want to upset other people, and Fives because they often don't realize that saying no is an option. Remember that you have the choice to say yes or no.

- If you feel offended, disrespected, unappreciated, or invaded, **pause to notice if one of your personal boundaries has been crossed.** Once you identify this boundary, ask yourself: How can I explicitly articulate this boundary to the person who crossed it?

- When you feel frustrated by a relationship, your tendency might be to pull back: to get quiet, change the subject, avoid the person, or even leave. But if you care about the relationship, you should know that these behaviors are unhelpful to you, because they communicate that you do not care. Instead, you can **ask yourself which boundary would allow you to continue the interaction or the relationship,** and then express that. For example, in a heated conversation, you can say, "I feel overwhelmed and need to take a break. Can we continue this conversation in an hour?"

- **Learn to use your voice in relationships that are important to you.** If you want your preferences to be appreciated, you need to express them. If you want someone to know how you feel about them, you need to tell them. If you want your boundaries to be respected, you need to assert them. And if you need help learning how to use your voice in relationships, you will need to ask for help.

The assertive stance

TYPE 3
THE LUMINARY

TYPE 7
THE EXPLORER

TYPE 8
THE WARRIOR

These types have an independent style of interaction. They take a direct approach to getting their needs met, moving directly ahead toward what they pursue, which sometimes entails moving against other people.

Threes move toward their goals and desired achievements, Sevens toward satisfaction and distraction, and Eights toward their own agenda and that which secures their independence. They don't mind pushing past obstacles and swimming upstream, but their energy and directness along the way can sometimes feel pushy or aggressive. These types don't have trouble asking for things or taking charge, so they are prone to overstepping other people's boundaries. When it comes to their own boundaries, they tend to be good at expressing them but have difficulty keeping them. They often push themselves too far, do too much, or move at high speed until they finally crash.

STARTING POINTS FOR HEALTHY BOUNDARIES

- **Practice being mindful of boundaries and notice when you cross them.** If you want to prioritize spending the weekend with your family, but you give your weekend time to someone or something else, you have disrespected your own boundary. If your employee states that they can't work more than 20 hours per week, but you schedule them for 24, you have disrespected their boundary.

- **Notice when you rush to someone's aid**—for example, to help them find solutions to their problems, to cheer them up and help them move on from painful emotions, or to protect them from bad decisions and situations. While none of these things are good or bad on their own, it's important to recognize when you are trying to fix a problem that is not yours to fix. Remember that it is ultimately more helpful if you empower someone to help themselves. Try moving from a stance of "Here, let me fix this for you" to "I have confidence in you that you can handle this."

- **Start asking for permission before offering advice or help.** If you want to cheer someone up, first ask, "How can I support you right now?" If you want to give someone advice, first ask, "Would you like to know what I think?" Honor the fact that their decisions and emotions belong to them.

- When you find yourself preoccupied with someone else's difficult emotions or problems, **ask yourself which difficult emotions or problems you are avoiding in your own life.** Learning to stop and feel your feelings will be helpful to you in your relationships.

- **Let go of your efforts to try to change other people.** Trying to change what other people think, feel, or do, will only leave you exhausted and frustrated. Practice putting your attention and energy into what you *can* change—your own behavior and choices.

Setting healthy boundaries

If you assert a boundary clearly, but someone consistently disregards it, you might need to assert a consequence for crossing that boundary. It must be something you are willing to follow through on and within your control, e.g., "If you continue yelling, I will not be able to continue this conversation."

POOR BOUNDARIES Blaming others for (or denying responsibility for) your own emotions, choices, needs, and preferences.	HEALTHY BOUNDARIES Taking responsibility for your own emotions, choices, needs, and preferences.
"Why are you so nosy?"	"I feel uncomfortable answering questions about my sex life."
"You don't make me feel loved."	"I've been feeling insecure in our relationship."
"Why didn't anyone order a gluten-free pizza option tonight?"	"I don't eat gluten. So I brought my own food tonight to make sure I'd have a dinner option."
"You're overreacting. I'm going for a walk."	"I feel overwhelmed and need to take a break. Can we continue this conversation in half an hour?"
"Sorry we keep missing each other, crazy week here!"	"I don't have time for a phone call this week. Can we talk next week?"
"You don't care what I think."	"I feel like my opinion isn't getting heard right now. But it's important to me that you understand what I'm thinking."
"It doesn't really matter what I think, does it?"	"I feel like my opinion doesn't get heard in our relationship as much as yours does. Would you be willing to ask me what I think more often?"
"Why didn't you tell me to quit my job sooner? You knew I was unhappy there."	"I was unhappy at my job, but I chose to continue working there for as long as I did."

POOR BOUNDARIES	HEALTHY BOUNDARIES
Taking responsibility for other people's emotions, choices, needs, and preferences.	Letting others take responsibility for their own emotions, choices, needs, and preferences.
"You definitely shouldn't do that. It's too risky."	"This is your choice, so your opinion matters most here. Let me know how I can support you."
"I talked to my friend about you...the one who's a marketing director. I know you didn't want me to, but it's just a really good connection to have. She said she can meet with you this Friday at 9am, so clear your schedule!"	"You sound very interested in marketing. Please tell me if you'd like me to connect you with my friend in marketing."
"I'm sorry for making you feel sad and jealous by wanting to hang out with my friends. I'll stay home with you instead."	"It's important to me that I hang out with my friends tonight. I love you. And I hope you can find a nice way to spend your evening."
"Sure, I can take your shift at work today. I was planning to go to my niece's birthday party, though. So maybe you can let me know if you find someone else."	"I'm sorry that you're hungover today and feel sick. But I am not able to work your shift."
"You shouldn't believe in that religion."	"I believe in something different. But I respect your right to have your own beliefs."
"You don't need to keep crying about that. It's not really a big deal and you'll feel better by tomorrow. Here, let me show you this funny video that will cheer you up!"	"I see that you're feeling sad. How can I support you right now?"
"You know that this disposable flatware you bought for your party is a bad choice for the environment, don't you? I can tell you which brand to get next time."	"Thank you for inviting me to your party."

TYPE

1

THE VISIONARY

Their decisions are
not my
responsibility.

TYPE

2

THE CONNECTOR

Their needs are not
my responsibility.

TYPE

3

THE LUMINARY

Their success is not
my responsibility.

TYPE

4

THE ARTIST

Their response to me
is not my
responsibility.

Healthy
boundary
mantras

These mantras are meant
to help you remember
where the boundary lines
are between you and
other people.
Remembering these lines
will help you care for
others (and yourself) out
of love and generosity
instead of obligation or
resentment.

TYPE
7
THE EXPLORER

Their happiness is not
my responsibility.

TYPE
6
THE ADVOCATE

Their choices are not
my responsibility.

TYPE
8
THE WARRIOR

Their safety is not my
responsibility.

TYPE
5
THE PHILOSOPHER

Their opinions are not
my responsibility.

TYPE
9
THE DIPLOMAT

Their comfort is not
my responsibility.

The three centers of wisdom

Your head, your heart, and your body: these are your centers of wisdom, the different ways that you experience life and process your experience. You have access to all three centers, but tend to use one more than the others.

Eights, Nines, and Ones operate primarily out of the body center and experience the world through intuition, sensing, and gut instinct. They share a common experience with anger.

Twos, Threes, and Fours operate primarily out of the heart center and experience life through their emotions and feelings. They share the key emotion of shame.

Fives, Sixes, and Sevens operate primarily out of the head center, experiencing life through thoughts and information. They share the emotion of fear.

Anger, shame, and fear are emotions that we each experience. But one of these emotions acts as a stronger force in your life than the others, determined by your primary center of wisdom.

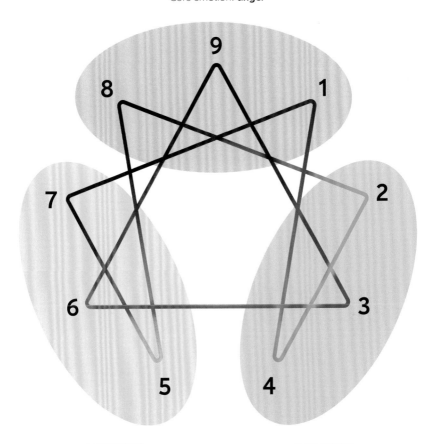

8•9•1

BODY CENTER

(doing, gut instinct, sensing, intuition)

Core emotion: **anger**

5•6•7

HEAD CENTER

(thinking, brain, information, logic)

Core emotion: **fear**

2•3•4

HEART CENTER

(feeling, soul, emotion, experiences)

Core emotion: **shame**

Head, heart, and body

- Each person has three centers of wisdom: head (thinking), heart (feeling), and body (sensing/intuiting).

- The three centers of wisdom are different ways to process and experience the world. None is superior to the others. They are all important and valid ways to experience the world and process your experience.

- Depending on your enneagram number, you use one of these centers more than the others. But you have the ability to use all three centers.

- You can underutilize or overutilize your center of wisdom, relying either too little or too much on your thoughts, your feelings, or your instincts. Ideally, all three centers will be used with balance.

- Learning about your center of wisdom will teach you important differences between the ways that you and your loved ones experience life and process events.

BODY CENTER: 8-9-1

The common emotion between numbers in the body center is anger. While Eights tend to outwardly express their anger, Nines ignore or fall asleep to their anger and are often not even aware of it until it boils over. And Ones internalize their anger, which might seep out as passive-aggression or stifled irritation. When you think of anger, think of the visceral way it fills up your body when you feel it. It brings a tangible heat with it, doesn't it? And it brings a force and a weight with it, too, doesn't it? This physical, body-centered experience is characteristic of types in the body center. Body center types move through the world with gut impulses that they either act on or suppress. These types tend to experience and process life through their perceptions, instincts and senses more than through conscious emotions or thoughts.

HEAD CENTER: 5-6-7

Fear is the common emotion between numbers in the head center. Fives retreat inward into their own internal experience, responding to a fear that they cannot competently navigate in the outside world. Sixes move toward outside sources of guidance and security, moving away from the internal fear that they won't make the right choices or that their safety will be threatened. And Sevens move toward what will fill their minds up with satisfaction and distraction, running from the internal fear that if they stop to feel their fear or their painful emotions, they will be overcome and not be okay. Think of what it's like to experience the emotion of fear, how it fills your headspace with thoughts of danger...or with thoughts to distract from thoughts of danger. Imagine how fear lights up your mind, telling it to stay on high alert. This is characteristic of head types, who process life primarily through thinking more than through feeling or sensing.

HEART CENTER: 2-3-4

Shame is the common emotion in the heart center. Shame is a deep insecurity that who you are is not good enough. Heart-centered types address this shame in different ways: Twos, by trying to win the affection of others, Threes by trying to earn the admiration of others, and Fours by trying to embody enough individuality and uniqueness to prove their own worth to themselves. Think of what it's like to experience the emotion of shame...the way this feeling moves like a wave across your heart... how it feels like dark clouds gathering in your soul. Picturing this type of emotional experience is key to understanding the feelings-oriented experience of heart-centered types, who live out of their emotions more than they do out of their thoughts or their gut instinct.

Centers of wisdom and relationships

- **Learn to honor the difference between the way you experience the world and the way others do.** If someone important to you has a different primary center of wisdom than you do, contemplate what it would be like to take in information and process experiences the way they do. This gives you a whole new way to see things from their perspective and understand where they're coming from.

- For deeper conversations, **ask questions that speak to all three centers of wisdom:**

  » What are your thoughts on this?

  » What does this feel like to you?

  » What is your gut instinct about this?

- **Before an important discussion, first process the topic using each of your centers of wisdom.** It's easy to react to others impulsively out of your primary center of wisdom alone. But if you express only your feelings, and the other person responds only with reason, you will be speaking different languages. Or if you express your thought process only, and they respond just with their gut instinct, you will, once again, be speaking different languages. Communication is more effective when you give each center of wisdom a place in the conversation.

- **Be careful not to disregard the importance of someone's primary center of wisdom.** Invalidating the importance of someone's emotional experience, intentional thought process, or intuition and gut-instinct is likely to lead to conflict...or at least some wounded feelings and frustration.

- **Knowing your primary center of wisdom can help you express your needs during joint decision-making.** If you are a heart type, you might need someone to show you that they understand the emotional impact of the decision. If you are a head type, you might need someone to affirm that they see the logic and rationality you are pointing to. And if you are a body type, you might need someone to acknowledge the gravity of your gut-level inclination about things, knowing that even though your gut-instinct about things might change, it needs space and time. Learning how to express these kinds of needs will help you communicate more effectively and peacefully during joint decisions.

- **During conflict, consider what key emotion might be driving your behavior.** If you are a heart type, what shame (the feeling that you are not acceptable as you are) is fueling your actions? If you are a body type, what anger is using this conflict as an outlet? And if you are a head type, what fear is lying beneath your thoughts and your reasoning? Acknowledging your own painful emotion can help you de-escalate yourself from an emotionally charged state so that helpful dialog can occur. If you choose to express your feelings out loud, just be sure to stick with "I feel" statements and avoid statements that blame the other person for your feelings.

REFERENCES

ACT Made Simple: An Easy-to-Read Primer on Acceptance and Commitment Therapy by Russ Harris

Authentic Happiness: Using the New Positive Psychology to Realize Your Potential for Lasting Fulfillment by Martin E.P. Seligman, PhD

Enneagraminstitute.com, created by Don Richard Riso and Russ Hudson

Feeling Good: The New Mood Therapy by David. D. Burns, MD

Get Out of Your Mind and Into Your Life: The New Acceptance and Commitment Therapy by Steven Hayes, PhD, with Spencer Smith

On Becoming a Person: A Therapist's View of Psychotherapy by Carl R. Rogers

The Complete Enneagram: 27 Paths to Greater Self-Knowledge by Beatrice Chestnut, PhD

The Mindful Self-Compassion Workbook: A Proven Way to Accept Yourself, Build Inner Strength, and Thrive by Kristin Neff, PhD

The Road Back to You by Ian Morgan Cron and Suzanne Stabile

The Wisdom of the Enneagram by Don Richard Riso and Russ Hudson

INDEX

PHOTO CREDITS

5 iStock: benedek. **8** Dreamstime.com: Robert Crum. **10-11** iStock: timnewman. **17** iStock: xenotar. **22** Getty RF: Arctic-Images. **26** Dreamstime.com: Dmitry Pichugin / Dmitryp. **64-65** iStock: Christian Petrone. **72** Dreamstime.com: Boule13. **91** iStock: FG Trade. **95** 123RF.com: subbotina. **106-107** iStock: 4nadia. **113** Dreamstime.com: Beatrice Preve. **116** iStock: AndrewSoundarajan.

ACKNOWLEDGMENTS

I am grateful to the enneagram teachers Suzanne Stabile, Ian Morgan Cron, Dr. Beatrice Chestnut, Don Richard Riso (1946–2012), and Russ Hudson, each of whom contributed to my understanding of and appreciation for the enneagram. And I am endlessly grateful to my family and my friends—whom I count as family—who empower me daily with their support, their input, their acceptance of me, and their belief in me.

ABOUT THE AUTHOR

Laura Miltenberger is the creator of *My Enneagram Journal* and the cofounder of @xoenneagram, an Instagram account providing resources for self-care and the enneagram. She currently resides in Portland, Oregon.